You Can Make It!

by Jim Bakker

PTL Television Network
Charlotte, North Carolina 28279

All scripture quotations in *You Can Make It* are taken from the King James Version of The Holy Bible unless otherwise indicated.

First Printing, 1983
Second Printing, 1985

ISBN 0-912275-00-6
© 1983 by PTL Enterprises, Inc.

PTL Television Network
Charlotte, North Carolina 28279

Printed in Canada

This book is dedicated to my beloved friend and pastor, Aubrey Sara.

...A man whose encouragement and support taught me to preach with victory, when I thought I'd preach no more.

...A man whose trust in the Lord inspired my faith, even in the face of heartache.

...A man whose loving spirit lives on today, in the countless hearts he touched during his sojourn here on earth.

Contents

Introduction

I felt like the end of the world had come.

Kneeling on the green carpet of the pastor's study, I sobbed my heart out. I was too ashamed to face the people — I was a failure...defeated before I got started. My spirit was crushed, and tears poured from my eyes in such a flood I couldn't even see.

Suddenly I became aware of someone's presence in the room, and I heard Tammy's concerned voice asking, "What's the matter, Jim?"

"I'll never preach again — it's all over." And sobs racked my body until I couldn't even talk. All I could do was cry.

Tammy left the room and came back in a few minutes with our host pastor, Aubrey Sara. Weeks before he'd met Tammy and me while holding a revival in our home church in Minneapolis, Minnesota. For some reason he'd taken a liking to us and invited two young, inexperienced kids to come hold our first revival in his church in North Carolina.

We had come with such high hopes — this was to be our launching pad into the ministry. I stepped into the pulpit and preached my heart out, expecting great results...a mighty move of the Spirit. When I stumbled through to the end of what I had to say and gave the invitation, the congregation just sat and stared at me. They were not moved...they had no reaction at all. I was devastated, because I'd been taught that the only way an evangelist could measure success was by results. By that standard I had failed completely.

And that's what I told Pastor Sara as he walked quietly into my pity party and looked down at me on the floor. "Brother Sara, I'm finished. I'm quitting the ministry."

1

A faint smile crossed his face, and he gently shook his head no. "Get up, son. You may think you preached the world's worst sermon, but you've got to leave the results with God. So you get out there and talk to the people.

"From now on when you finish preaching, you hold your head high and walk to the front door. Look people straight in the eye and shake hands with them as they leave the church."

"Then, you don't think I should quit the ministry?"

He chuckled, and shook his head again. "Just trust the Lord and see what happens."

Sure enough, before the revival was over, God gave us a real breakthrough among the young people, and the Holy Spirit ministered in a beautiful way. At the end of the meeting, many people testified that they had been saved and filled with the Holy Spirit, and many others reported that they had been healed of physical afflictions. With Pastor Sara's encouragement and God's help, we made it through our first revival.

Pastor Sara became a spiritual father to Tammy and me. We stayed in his home often and learned much about ministering — about living — from his quiet, yet forceful example. After that first revival in his church, he called other pastors and urged them to schedule Jim and Tammy Bakker for revivals. He even drove us to some of our meetings. His loving support never wavered. His belief in us gave us the confidence to keep going.

It was Pastor Sara who helped me become a licensed minister. And it was Pastor Sara who always had good advice and encouraging words when we called from time to time with our problems and concerns. When he felt we needed defending at various times in our years of ministry, we found him to be an unyielding ally and staunch friend.

When we began working with Christian television, not everyone was as enthusiastic about our vision of harnessing modern technology for God's work as we were. One of the things that kept us going was the knowledge that Pastor Sara understood what we saw...and believed in our dream. "Just trust the Lord, Jim, and see what happens."

Aubrey Sara was no stranger to heartache and adversity. Often it seemed tragedy stalked his life. His wife was stricken with a crippling disease but had a dramatic healing and a full recovery. Later, another killing disease took her life.

One of his sons was deserted by his wife and was left to care for two youngsters. Soon after that, he was killed in a grisly train-car accident, and the children became wards of the court, placed in a state institution. Pastor Sara went and got the boys and raised them in his own home.

His heart seemed to go out to the underdog, the down and out. He established a boys ranch in Florida for mistreated and abused youngsters and was an active force to influence legislation in that state to protect them.

During all his trials, Pastor Sara kept smiling. His devotion and faith in God never wavered. He was steady as a rock...always concerned more for others than himself.

Naturally, when the time came to establish a church at Heritage USA to serve as the spiritual heart for the entire PTL ministry, Tammy and I thought of Pastor Sara. And he agreed to join us as an associate minister and direct the day-to-day operation of the church. Although I preached on Sunday whenever I could, Pastor Sara kept everything running smoothly. He was

3

always there when I couldn't be...he preached the midweek services...he was a kind and capable overseer of all activities...he counseled with the troubled and needy.

And he was always eager to listen when I needed to talk to someone. I could pour out my heart to him when I was discouraged, upset, or uncertain. Somehow he always knew when to just listen and when to make me listen to his godly counsel. He was a constant source of positive support and encouragement.

When God showed me I was to build a replica of the Upper Room at Heritage USA, Pastor Sara was as excited about it as I was. He watched each step of the construction with keen interest. Perhaps more than anyone else he understood the significance of this place. The "original" Upper Room in Jerusalem was where the power of the Holy Spirit fell upon the first believers on the day of Pentecost. It was God's way of saying, *"YOU CAN MAKE IT."*

Although he had been in poor health for several months, and had even suffered a slight stroke, Pastor Sara became the first pastor of the Upper Room at Heritage USA. He directed all the staff ministers who served in the Upper Room (someone is on duty there 24 hours a day, ready to pray, anoint with oil, and to serve the Lord's Supper twice a day).

When the Upper Room was dedicated on July 4, 1982, we began a period of intensive intercession for the needs of our partners. For 120 days we prayed for those who wrote, keeping their requests in the Upper Room.

But before the 120 days of prayer were completed, God called his servant, Aubrey Sara, to be with Him. Pastor Sara was stricken with a cerebral hemorrhage on August 26, 1982, and died a few hours later.

He was a good man. He was a giving man. He never stopped giving and he never stopped loving.

4

He was buried just outside the Upper Room he loved so much. Before his funeral, his body lay in state inside that simple place of prayer.

Tammy and I went to spend a few minutes alone with him there. As we looked at the earthly remains of this great man who had been such a strong influence on our ministry and our lives, it seemed we could almost hear him saying, "Just keep on trusting the Lord and see what happens."

I squeezed my wife's hand and said, "Well, Tammy, I guess we're going to have to grow up now."

Hebrews 12 speaks of our being compassed about with a great cloud of witnesses—great heroes of faith who have gone before us and who are looking down at our progress, cheering us on. Sometimes when I look up to heaven I can almost see them with my spiritual eyes.

Now when the going gets rough and I look up to heaven for a little encouragement, I know I'll be able to "see" Pastor Sara watching, and I'll hear his quiet voice saying, "Get up, Jim, and keep on going—*you can make it!*

This book is dedicated to the memory of my friend and pastor, Aubrey Sara. And if you've ever needed to be reminded that you can make it, this book is also dedicated to you.

—*Jim Bakker*

Chapter One
God Wants You To Make It

The first words God ever spoke to man on the newly-created earth were, "I want you to make it!"

You can read it for yourself in the first chapter of Genesis. The Bible tells the amazing story of creation, how God spoke into existence the heavens and the earth, the planets and stars, the plants and animals. Then He created man — *"in the image of God created he him"* (Genesis 1:27).

But the very next verse sets the stage for man's role on the earth and reveals God's will for all human kind, including you and me. God spoke these thrilling words to His first man, His highest creation:

"Be fruitful, and multiply, and replenish the earth, and subdue it: and have dominion...over every living thing that moveth upon the earth."

What a paradise Adam was given in the Garden of Eden. He was master of all he surveyed, as far as he could see, in every direction. Every plant that grew was his to use as he saw fit, and the abundant fruit of all the orchards was his to enjoy—except for the fruit of a single tree. The fruit from the tree of the knowledge of good and evil he was to avoid upon pain of death.

The Bible says God brought all the animals and birds He created to Adam, and whatever he called them became their name. The man was put in charge of all creation.

Then the Lord made Adam a companion, "an help meet." And together they enjoyed the fullness of the

6

good life. All day long they worked together in the Garden of Eden, tending and caring for it. And at the end of the day God himself would come down to walk in the garden in the cool of the evening and have fellowship with man.

Someone has said that Adam didn't have to make it — he already had it made!

But, of course, the situation changed. We all know the story of how the serpent tempted the woman to taste the forbidden fruit. "But God says we'll die if we eat of that tree," she argued.

"You won't die," said the serpent. "God told you that because He knows eating that fruit will make you like Him, knowing good from evil."

So she ate the fruit and took some to Adam, and he ate it too. Instantly their eyes were opened, and for the first time they realized they were naked. Right away they made aprons, or clothes, to cover themselves.

Notice the next thing that happened. God came back to have fellowship with them again. You see, from the beginning of human history, God has desired to be man's friend. He has wanted him to have good things, the best of everything. Most of all, He wanted to walk with him, talk with him, commune with him.

But when God came into the garden this time, Adam and Eve were nowhere to be found. The Bible says they *"hid themselves from the presence of the Lord God"* (Genesis 3:8).

The birth of death

God knew what had happened. He called out to His beloved creation, the man He had delighted to have fellowship with — *"Where are you?"*

Adam and his wife came slinking out of the bushes to face the Friend who had become their Judge. They responded to His questions in a manner that has become one of man's most familiar traits down through the centuries.

"Adam, did you disobey Me and eat of the forbidden fruit?"

"Well, it wasn't really my fault, Lord. The woman You gave me brought it to me or I never would have touched it!"

"Woman, what have you done?"

"Now don't go blaming me. It wasn't my idea — the serpent tricked me into doing it."

Sound familiar? Have you ever tried to defend your guilt by "passing the buck"? Have any of your kids ever tried to pull this trick on you? Did it work?

It didn't for Adam and Eve, either. God pronounced judgment upon Adam and Eve and the serpent. On that day, mankind's physical immortality came to an end as death came into the world. From that day on Adam and Eve began to die!

No longer would the earth give up its treasures to man as a free gift. Adam would have to struggle and toil in the sun to cultivate the land and harvest a food crop amid the thorns and thistles. The Living Bible puts it this way — *"All your life you will sweat to master it, until your dying day"* (Genesis 3:19).

No longer would new life come to the earth as a result of the spoken Word and creative power of God. Instead, Eve would undergo the pain and travail of childbirth and be subject to her husband.

To the serpent, God prophesied that he would be forever cursed, feared, and despised. Also, a limit was placed on his ability to hurt mankind. Speaking of the Son of Man who would come, born of a woman, to be mankind's Saviour, God said, *"You will bruise His heel but He will bruise your head."*

8

Adam and Eve were forced out of the beautiful Garden of Eden and into a world that would sustain them only through struggle and hard work. Mankind had passed into a new era.

Some people have misinterpreted the punishment meted out to mankind in this account to mean that man was totally rejected by God and was completely powerless and defeated from that day on. But that's just not true. God didn't stop loving man. He didn't give up on him and discard him. He wasn't through blessing him or using him. Regardless of man's disobedience, God still desired to reestablish communion with man and have fellowship with him.

I love the song Tammy sings that says, *"God's not through blessing you...never give up, what He says, He will do!"* God's love doesn't change. He speaks to every human heart a message of hope — "You can make it."

The fourth chapter of Genesis tells the sad story of Adam's son Cain, who grew violently angry because his sacrifice of farm produce was rejected by God. His brother Abel's sacrifice of young lambs had been accepted. (Sacrifices to God always have had to be blood sacrifices because blood symbolizes life.)

But even in the midst of Cain's anger, when jealousy and hatred for his brother was rising, God tried to help him. The Living Bible gives this account: *"Why are you angry?" the Lord asked him. "Why is your face so dark with rage? It can be bright with joy if you will do what you should! But if you refuse to obey, watch out. Sin is waiting to attack you, longing to destroy you. But you can conquer it!"* (Genesis 4:6, 7).

You can conquer it! You can make it! That was God's promise to Cain. And it is His message to you today.

Unfortunately, Cain failed to heed God's voice. Instead of conquering sin, he willfully gave in to it. Taking Abel out into the fields, Cain attacked and killed his brother.

Cain had been a farmer, a man of the soil. As his punishment, God made him leave his farm and become a man without a country, a fugitive and a wanderer for the rest of his life. The saddest part of Cain's story is that it did not have to turn out that way. He could have been happy and successful. God wanted him to make it!

Starting over— man's new opportunity

One of the most graphic stories of God's will for man is the story of Noah. Every child in Sunday School learns about Noah and his giant ark filled with all kinds of animals and birds. But the reason Noah and his family ended up in that floating zoo was to carry out God's plan for man to make it.

Several hundred years after the time of Adam and Eve, God saw that the entire human race had become wicked. The Bible says men were so evil that God was sorry He had made them — their wickedness broke His heart. And God decided He would destroy them all... blotting them off the face of the earth.

Then He remembered Noah, the only righteous man living. Noah had always tried to live in a way that was pleasing to God.

So God, in the midst of His sorrow and anger, made a way for Noah to make it. He instructed Noah to build a huge boat to float his family above the flood that was coming to the earth to destroy all the wicked. Noah was to build the ark large enough to preserve enough pairs of animals to repopulate the world all over again.

It was not an easy assignment. Noah and his sons

10

must have labored long and hard to build a wooden boat 450 feet long, 75 feet wide, and 45 feet high (see Genesis 6:15). But Noah was determined to make it...and he refused to give up.

Even when his family and all the animals were aboard the ark and the rains began, "making it" must have been quite an ordeal. As nearly as I can figure from what the Bible says, from the time the 40 days and nights of rain began until the flood waters receded and the earth dried up enough for Noah and all the animals to come out, they had been cooped up together for about 14 months! If you've ever driven your family across country on vacation and been in the car together for two or three days, you've probably got a little idea of what Noah must have gone through.

But he made it! No one else in the whole world survived. Everything and everybody else was destroyed. But God brought Noah through.

The reminder of the rainbow

Then God said to Noah, "Let's start over. Go out and repopulate the earth and subdue it. I'm putting you in charge of all the animals and everything in the world. And I promise I'll never destroy the world again with a flood. I'll even give you a sign of My promise — a rainbow. When the clouds come, look for My rainbow. It will remind you that I have not forgotten My promise."

Everytime you see a rainbow, remember that it is God saying, "You can make it. I won't destroy your world but will help you make it through."

All through the Bible, God tried to make people understand that He was on their side — that He wanted them to be winners. But it seems that people invariably try to make God their adversary. Trials come — they blame God. Hard times make life unpleasant and

11

someone says, "God must be trying to tell us something." Tragedy strikes, and newspapers and insurance companies call it "an act of God."

I used to be literally terrified of God. When I was just a small child, someone put up a large black and white picture of a human eye in my Sunday School classroom — it must have been three feet across. To me, that eye was God himself, and He was looking directly at me.

We were taught a kids' song that warned, *"Be careful little feet where you go...be careful little eyes what you see...be careful little tongue what you say..."* Every time I sang that song I felt uncomfortable. I knew the big "Eye" was always looking and was just waiting for me to make a mistake so He could get me.

No one ever made me understand that God wanted to help me, not punish me. It never dawned on me that He wanted me to make it, not to fail. And over the years I've discovered that lots of other people had a similar experience in their first concept of God. In fact, there are still millions of people cringing through life just hoping God won't notice them and swat them off the face of the earth.

If only we could see what God is really like. If only we could understand that He love us...just the way we are, right or wrong. If only we could hear His voice saying, "You can make it because, no matter what happens, "I'm here to help you!"

Life is never going to be effortless. You can't get to the top by walking on level ground all the time. Bad times come to everybody, saint and sinner alike. God never promised that you wouldn't have to go through the valley — just that you wouldn't have to go through it alone. *"I will never leave thee, nor forsake thee,"* He declares (Hebrews 13:5). "With Me by your side, you can make it."

God will make a way for you—even in bad times

Joseph knew what it was to face hardship and betrayal. His own brothers turned against him. Now, to be fair about it, Joseph was his father Jacob's pet. And he was pretty cocky about it, bragging about some dreams he had that suggested his brothers should bow down to him. But that's hardly a "killing" offense.

Yet, when Joseph went out to check on his brothers and the flocks they were tending, his brothers decided to kill him and throw his body down a well. Then one brother got soft-hearted and said, "Well, let's not kill him — we'll just throw him in the well and let him die by himself."

So they did that. They took off Joseph's dandy little coat of many colors their father had given him to show he was the favorite. They decided to sprinkle it with a goat's blood and show it to Jacob, saying that a wild animal must have eaten him.

While they were scheming, a caravan of traders came by. One of the other brothers said, "Hey, I've got an even better idea than letting old Dreamy starve in that dry well — let's sell him into slavery. We'll get rid of him and make a profit to boot!"

A few pieces of silver changed hands, and Joseph was on his way to Egypt, wearing the chains of bondage. In a matter of minutes he had gone from daddy's pet to a lowly slave!

I don't know what Joseph's reaction was. The Bible doesn't tell us. But if this had happened to some people I know they'd have whined, "I give up. What's the use? Why me, Lord? What did I ever do to make You hate me so much?" They'd have moaned and taken on so that they would not have heard the still small voice of the

Lord saying, "I'll make a way for you even in Egypt — you can make it!"

Joseph was bought by an Egyptian named Potiphar, who was the captain of the Pharoah's guards. This man put him to work in his house. Joseph did such a good job that he was soon promoted. He worked his way up to being manager of Potiphar's entire household, including his business affairs. God helped him to make it!

But Joseph's troubles weren't over. He was a fine looking young man, and Potiphar's wife began making eyes at him. In fact, she asked him to come to her bed.

Joseph refused. "My master trusts me with everything he owns. How could I do this wicked thing against him and God?"

Then one day this temptress came to Joseph when no one else was around and demanded that he commit adultery with her. He tried to make a run for it...to get away from her. I believe it was Shakespeare who wrote, "Hell hath no fury like a woman scorned." As Joseph turned to leave, Mrs. Potiphar grabbed his sleeve and hung on, pulling his whole jacket off. Then she screamed, "Rape!"

You guessed it — Joseph ended up in the dungeon. After all, who's going to take the word of a slave over that of the wife of the captain of the guard?

I'm sure Joseph must have been pretty discouraged. When you try hard and do the best you can and bad things just keep on happening, it's hard to keep your chin up. But even in that dismal situation, God stayed close to Joseph. He kept on telling him, "You can make it."

The chief jailer took a liking to Joseph. For one thing, he didn't cause any trouble...and he was willing to do some extra work. He proved himself to be trustworthy. Before long, Joseph was doing most of the chief jailer's work, and all the other prisoners were responsible to him. Even in prison, Joseph was able to make it.

Interpreting dreams to save a nation

One day two of the Pharoah's servants were thrown into the dungeon, and Joseph was responsible for taking care of them. After some time, the two men both woke up one morning worrying about the dreams they'd had the night before.

Joseph was able to interpret both the dreams. He told one man, the wine taster, that in three days he would be released from prison and given his old job back. The other man, the baker, would be executed in three days. Both predictions came true.

The wine taster promised to tell the Pharoah about Joseph and try to get him released when he went back to work. But he forgot all about it, and two long years went by.

Then the Pharoah had some troubling dreams. He could not figure out what they meant, and none of the sages and wise men of Egypt could either. The Pharoah was greatly concerned and troubled, for he was sure the dreams had some important meaning he should know about.

Suddenly the wine taster remembered Joseph and how he had interpreted his dream and the baker's dream two years before. He told the Pharoah, and Joseph was summoned. Genesis 41 relates how he was able to interpret the dreams, which both had the same meaning. One involved seven sleek, fat cows which were eaten by seven gaunt, ugly cows. The second dream was about a grain stalk with seven full, plump heads. Another stalk, with seven withered, blighted heads sprang up and consumed the good heads of grain.

Joseph explained that the fat cows and healthy grain represented seven years of plenty — the scrawny cows and withered heads of grain represented seven years of famine. But the famine would be so severe that the seven years of abundance would be forgotten.

Then Joseph recommended that the Pharoah select a wise man to store 20 percent of the abundant crops in each of the first seven years so there would be enough food on hand to see the nation through the following seven years of famine. The Pharoah thought that was a good idea — and he chose Joseph!

The Pharoah took off his signet ring and put it on Joseph's hand. He dressed him in fine clothes, put a gold chain around his neck, and gave him a royal chariot. He said, "You have authority over the entire nation, second only to me. No man can lift a hand or a foot without your consent!"

So Joseph went out to govern Egypt...and just the day before he had been a foreign slave in a prison dungeon!

Don't tell me your circumstances are too difficult to overcome. Don't tell me you're going to give up because there is just no hope, no way out. Your situation is no worse than Joseph's was, and he made it! God moved him from prison to the palace in just one day! God lifted him from being a lowly slave and made him ruler of the most powerful nation on earth.

Joseph's God is your God too!

And what He did for Joseph, He will do for you.

So don't ever say, "I can't make it — I'm too sinful, too sick, too discouraged, too much in debt, too defeated." God is ready to get on your case, and He's never failed yet. He has a plan for your life...and that plan is good.

You can make it.

God meant it for good!

Joseph's interpretation of the Pharoah's dreams was exactly right. There were seven years of plenty and prosperity in Egypt. And Joseph appointed officers to take the surplus food and grain and store it in all the cities across the nation.

Then came the famine. There was not enough rain. The fields were parched and dry. Crops were meager at first — then non-existent. People accustomed to plenty used up all their reserves, then began to panic. Many cried out to the Pharoah for bread.

He told the people, "Go to Joseph and do what he tells you."

Joseph and his men opened the storehouses across the nation and provided grain for the people. There was enough stored up to supply everybody's need.

In fact, there was enough to sell to people from the countries around Egypt which were also suffering from the famine. One day over in Canaan, Jacob called his sons together and said, "I've heard there is grain in Egypt — go buy some for us before we all starve."

Now these were the same rascals who had sold their brother Joseph into slavery years before. Isn't it ironic that now they followed him to Egypt and bowed down before him — just as he had dreamed many years before in their father's house!

They didn't recognize Joseph...but he knew them instantly. And instead of taking revenge upon them, he provided the food they needed to save all their families from starvation.

You see, there was a purpose for Joseph's promotion and position. God helped him to make it for a reason. The last chapter of Genesis sums it up beautifully. When Joseph's brothers came begging forgiveness for the great evil they did to him, he wept. Then he said, *"Ye thought evil against me; but God meant it unto good, to bring to pass as it is this day, to save much people alive."* (Genesis 50:20).

Don't ever forget that God has a purpose in what you are going through. The adversity may not make any sense to you. In your heartache and pain you may feel that God has forgotten you. You may not see how any good can come from your predicament.

But God knows exactly where you are and what you need. No matter who lets you down or turns against you, God is still your friend. Your enemies may plot against you and try to hurt you, but God will keep you and shield you from destruction. Others may intend evil in what comes your way, but God means it for your good.

God wants you to make it. How do I know...how can I be so sure? Because He said so in His Word. Look at this — *"For I know the thoughts that I think toward you, saith the Lord, thoughts of peace, and not of evil, to give you an expected end"* (Jeremiah 29:11).

I tell you, God is for you, not against you. And with Him on your side, you cannot be defeated. He is thinking good thoughts about you, wanting good things for you — and He'll move heaven and earth to help you make it!

But once you've "made it," that's not the end of it. It's really the beginning. Your new prosperity, or health, or knowledge, your new confidence and courage, your new resources are not for you alone. They are to make it possible for you to help someone else — as Joseph said, "to save many people."

So if the night seems dark, my friend, know that a new morning is about to dawn.

As my friend, Oral Roberts says, "God is going to rain on your desert!"

18

Peace is going to overshadow your troubled heart. Healing is on the way to restore your body. Prosperity is coming to supply your every need. God wants you to make it. And because He does... YOU CAN MAKE IT!

Chapter Two

Putting First Things First

When you hear me say, "You can make it," what does that mean to you?

What does it mean to "make it"? Can you define that phrase or explain what people are talking about when they say that a particular individual "has it made"?

I've discovered it often means different things to different people —

A medical team and a frightened family keep a worried vigil to see if a critically ill patient will "make it" through the night...

A runner in a long distance race pushes himself to the absolute limit of his endurance to "make it" to the finish line...

An exhausted laborer uses his last bit of strength and energy to "make it" to the end of the day...

And most of us know — or remember all too well — what it's like to scrimp and scrape just to "make it" through those last few days before payday.

Usually, the person who "has it made" possesses something we don't have but admire and desire — whether it be money, prestige, power, position, talent, etc. And many times our envy is terribly short-sighted.

One day a hobo sat by his campfire, eating a can of pork-and-beans, when he saw a long, sleek limousine carrying a millionaire businessman go by. "Just look at that," said the hobo. "Fancy car, fancy clothes, probably on his way to some fancy restaurant — that guy has really got it made!"

20

Inside the car, the millionaire took another pill to ease the pain of his ulcer and said to his chauffeur, "Did you see that guy — no worries, no responsibilities, doing anything he wants...he's really got it made. And I'd give anything to be able to eat pork-and-beans from a can and live to tell about it!"

See what I mean? Your idea of "having it made" or being able to "make it" and another person's idea may well be entirely different.

The truth is, from time to time all of us get our sense of values out of focus and our priorities mixed up. We tend to neglect the important things and spend too much time majoring in minors. But if we are to "make it" — if we are to be successful in any part of life — we must learn to put first things first.

Soon after Jesus began His earthly ministry, He was teaching in a house in the city of Capernaum. A great crowd gathered to hear Him, for they had heard of the miracles He performed and the way He spoke with authority. In a short time the house was jammed with people, and those who came later couldn't even get near the door.

The gospel of Mark tells how four men came to the house bringing a paralyzed man on a stretcher. When they saw they couldn't get through the crowd, they went up on the roof and cut a hole above where Jesus was. Then they let their friend down into the room.

What a dramatic moment! Here is Jesus, the miracle worker, standing at the side of a paralyzed man. The crowd looks on, breathless with anticipation. The man's friends peer down from the roof, knowing that Jesus can meet his great need.

The Master looked down at the man and said, *"Son, thy sins be forgiven thee"* (Mark 2:5).

Can you imagine how shocked everybody must

have been? *Sins forgiven?* The religious leaders looking on were indignant the Jesus would be so blasphemous as to suggest He could forgive sins — something only God can do. Everybody else was shocked that Jesus was more interested in the man's soul than his helpless, paralyzed body. They were expecting Jesus to deal with the man's obvious physical problem and heal his body.

The greatest miracle

Jesus took this opportunity to teach some important lessons. To the scribes, He sought to reveal who He really was — the divine Son of God. To those who came to see miracles, He demonstrated that the greatest miracle of all is the salvation of a human soul! To the paralyzed man, He declared, "You can make it...by putting first things first."

One thing is for certain — Jesus certainly got everybody's attention. And once He had forgiven the man's sins, He said, *"But that ye may know that the Son of man hath power on earth to forgive sins..."* Then He looked back at the sick man and said, *"Arise, and take up thy bed, and go thy way into thine house."*

Immediately the man was healed. He got up, picked up his bed and started for home. Everyone he passed on the way was amazed and said, "We've never seen anything like this before!" (TLB).

The lesson is clear — the condition of your soul is far more important than the condition of your body. That doesn't mean God isn't interested in your physical needs — He did heal the paralytic after He forgave his sins. But He puts first things first. Your eternal life is far more important than any concern of this life. Nothing is as important as your salvation — your personal relationship with God through our Saviour, the Lord Jesus Christ.

Luke tells of 70 disciples Jesus commissioned to go out 2 by 2 as evangelists. They returned from their mission, thrilled to report that even demons were subject to them in the name of the Lord.

Jesus said, *"Rejoice not, that the spirits are subject unto you; but rather rejoice, because your names are written in heaven"* (Luke 10:20).

Again and again Jesus reminded His followers that a person's soul is far more valuable than any possessions he may have or any riches he may seek. *"For what shall it profit a man, if he shall gain the whole world, and lose his own soul?"* (Mark 8:36).

Perhaps you're thinking, "There's no danger of my getting rich or having so much it would affect my spiritual life. But on the other hand, I do have to make a living. I don't have time to attend every church service or religious meeting that comes along. I can't watch every Christian TV program or read all the books and listen to all the tapes that come out. My family has to have a place to live, clothes to wear, food to eat. Are you telling me that religion is more important than those responsibilities?"

No indeed! Your family's needs are vitally important. I don't believe it would be pleasing to God for you to neglect those responsibilities. But that's not what Jesus asks. He simply says to keep your priorities straight — to put first things first.

In the Sermon on the Mount, Jesus said, *"Therefore take no thought, saying, What shall we eat? or, What shall we drink? or, wherewithal shall we be clothed?...for your heavenly Father knoweth that ye have need of all these things. But seek ye first the kingdom of God, and his righteousness; and all these things shall be added unto you"* (Matthew 6:31-33).

Seek first the kingdom

You can make it...in your finances, your career, your family — in everything — if you first get your heart right with God and keep the lines of communication open between Him and you. Being a Christian — a child of God — is the foundation on which the entire "You can make it" concept and structure is based. Because without God, you CAN'T make it!

If you aren't where you want to be in life, the first thing to do is check your personal relationship with God. Do you know beyond a shadow of a doubt that God is your Father and the Lord Jesus Christ is your Saviour, Friend, and Brother? Being sure of your personal salvation is the starting place for achieving any real and lasting success in life.

Here's the simple, straightforward "good news" of the gospel — God loves you, He really does! He loves you so much that He sent His own Son to pay the penalty for your sins and bring you back into a loving relationship with Him.

You see, even after "starting over" with mankind through Noah after the flood, God never enjoyed the close personal communion with these later generations of men that He'd had with Adam in the Garden of Eden. Not only did man continue to separate himself from his creator, over the centuries he lost sight of the true nature of God. Instead of recognizing Him as Father and Friend, man perceived God as an all-powerful tyrant, demanding and stern.

Finally, men either rebelled against God as they imagined Him to be or cowered before Him in fear and despair. At this dismal point in human history, God sent His Son Jesus into the world. He sent Him to show men what God is really like — that He is loving and generous and kind...that He does not want to punish man but to save him.

That's why John 3:16 is known as the Golden Text of the Bible. It is the unmistakable declaration of God's will toward you and me...a perfect portrait of our loving heavenly Father. It is a hand-carried, personally-delivered letter to us from God that says, "You can make it!"

Read it over again with new understanding and new appreciation: *"For God so loved the world, that he gave his only begotten Son, that whosoever believeth in him should not perish, but have everlasting life."*

And look at verse 17's tremendous truth — *"For God sent not his Son into the world to condemn the world; but that the world through him might be saved."*

Every person Jesus met, He forgave!

Jesus came to seek and to save the lost. He came in love and forgiveness, not vengeance and punishment. Throughout the New Testament Jesus dealt with sinners in love and changed their lives. He hated their sin, but loved them. There was no life so ruined He could not make it over. There was no deed so terrible He could not forgive.

Zacchaeus was a cheating, dishonest tax collector. But when he met Jesus he became a saint. He gave back what he had taken wrongfully and shared what he had left with the poor.

The Samaritan woman at the well had lived a life of shame and immorality. But when she accepted the "living water" Jesus offered, she became pure and clean — a new creation in Christ.

The woman taken in adultery expected only death by stoning as the cruel penalty for her sins. But when she looked into the face of Jesus, she found forgiveness and the strength and courage to begin life over again.

The power Jesus had then He still has today.

And what He did for those people He will do for you.

The words He proclaimed to a multitude on a hillside overlooking the Sea of Galilee come ringing over the centuries to you today — *"Blessed are they which do hunger and thirst after righteousness: for they shall be filled"* (Matthew 5:6). Do you know what that means? That is God saying in yet another way — "You can make it!"

During His earthly ministry, Jesus often used parables to teach those who gathered about Him. The fifteenth chapter of Luke records three interesting parables about lostness — and being found.

First, Jesus told about a shepherd who lost one of his sheep, probably when it wandered away from the herd and was unable to find its way back. The shepherd left his other 99 sheep and went out into the wilderness to look for the one that was lost. When he found it, crying and afraid, he placed it on his shoulder and carried it home. Then he called all his friends to rejoice with him because the lost was found.

Next, Jesus related a story about a housewife who had 10 silver pieces and discovered that one of the coins was missing. She lit a candle and began to clean the house thoroughly, sweeping in every corner, looking until she found the coin. She, too, invited her neighbors to rejoice with her that the lost was found.

Then the Lord told what is probably the best known of all His parables, the story of the prodigal son. A young man demands his inheritance, goes away from his family, and wastes all the money. Destitute and in despair, he comes to his senses and decides to return to his father's house to ask for a job as a servant. But on the way back, "when he was yet a great way off," the father saw him and ran to welcome him with a kiss. He cleaned him up, gave him new garments, and prepared a feast to celebrate the return of his son.

Jesus seemed to be saying that people can get lost in different ways. Some, like the coin, seem to be the victim of circumstances, such as environment, education, home atmosphere, or attitude of parents. Others, like the sheep, simply wander away and can't find their way back again. But perhaps most of us are like the prodigal son who deliberately chose to be lost — we even go to great lengths to cut ourselves off from God and those who love us most.

But in every one of Jesus' examples, no one wanted the lost to stay that way — not the shepherd, the woman, the father. The first two went and searched for the lost until they found them. And as soon as the prodigal showed that he no longer wanted to be lost, the father went to receive him...while he was still a long way off.

And with the sheep, the coin, and the son, there was great rejoicing when they were found. Jesus was saying, "God wants you to be saved — His heart is filled with joy when you come back into fellowship with Him."

Maybe you never intended to be lost and separated from God. Perhaps you were just going to explore the wilderness of sin a little bit and come right back, but you lost your way. Or, you may have deliberately cut yourself off from God...and found only emptiness and shame in your far country. Whatever your experience, God does not want you to be lost.

Don't let Satan deceive you

The devil tries to make sin seen so attractive and appealing. Sin seems to offer bright lights, the big beat, excitement, glamour, fun. Movies, magazines, and television all show the stars, the beautiful people on the fast track with alcohol, drugs, sex — the endless high, the ever-bigger thrill.

Sometimes these temptations are hard to resist, especially for young people who have not fully experienced the realities of life. Many are deceived by thinking of all they would have to "give up" to serve God.

But Satan doesn't want you to see behind the scenes at what a life of sin is really like. He doesn't show you his stars spending endless hours in dirty dressing rooms and dreary motels, lying sick in their own vomit or sticking needles in their arms to get "up" enough to keep on going for one more night, one more show.

The devil doesn't want to talk about the misery of alcoholism that ruins health, wipes out careers, stamps out marital love, and abuses children — or the horror a drunken driver feels when he wakes up after the crash to learn he has murdered one, two, three — perhaps several — innocent people.

And in the heat of lust, who thinks of the awful price being paid for a moment of passion? No one expects to feel so guilty, so ashamed...so dirty. No one intends for those he really loves to be hurt. No one expects to end up *diseased* — permanently marked with an insidious infection like herpes for which medical science can find no cure!

But it happens — every day it happens. Let me be completely blunt about the sin of fornication and adultery. The vulgar slang expression often used for the sex act or partner is "piece." In a sense, it is an apt term because each time a person is involved in an illicit sexual act, he or she is literally breaking off a piece of himself, a piece of his mind, a piece of his body, a piece of his soul — and destroying it forever.

Tell me, would you be willing to "give up" this side of sin's bargain to serve God? Are you willing to be rescued and set free from the cruel bondage of the devil? Are you willing to be saved and reunited in fellowship with God?

One of the clearest paths to salvation is found in the apostle Paul's letter to the Romans, in a remarkable series of verses Christian leaders often call "the Roman road." Here it is in its simple clarity, from the Living Bible:

"Yes, all have sinned; all fall short of God's glorious ideal...For the wages of sin is death, but the free gift of God is eternal life through Jesus Christ our Lord...But God showed his great love for us by sending Christ to die for us while we were still sinners...Anyone who calls upon the name of the Lord will be saved...For if you tell others with your own mouth that Jesus Christ is your Lord, and believe in your own heart that God has raised him from the dead, you will be saved...So there is now no condemnation awaiting those who belong to Christ Jesus...And so, dear brothers, I plead with you to give your bodies to God. Let them be a living sacrifice, holy — the kind he can accept. When you think of what he has done for you, is this too much to ask? Don't copy the behavior and customs of this world, but be a new and different person with a fresh newness in all you do and think. Then you will learn from your own experience

how his ways will really satisfy you" (Romans 3:23, 6:23, 5:8, 10:13, 10:9, 8:1, 12:1, 2).

Perhaps you've already discovered that you don't like what you're getting out of life. You've tried all the things you thought would give you satisfaction and found only emptiness and disappointment.

You may even feel that you've already ruined your life, that your mistakes and sins have done too much damage to repair.

Well, I have good news for you. God loves you. He is able to pick up the shattered pieces of your broken dreams and put them together again. The blood of our Saviour can wash away your sins and make your heart as white as snow. The love of God will forgive you of every one of your transgressions.

Pray the sinner's prayer with me

I urge you to settle the sin question in your life once and for all by asking Jesus to forgive you and give you a whole new life in Him. If you really want to make it, both in this life and the world to come, this is the first step. Right where you are, stop and pray this simple sinner's prayer with me:

"O God, I know that I am a sinner, lost and away from Your presence. Through the blood of Your Son Jesus, forgive me for all my sins, all my faults and failures that have kept me in bondage to the devil's power. Take away my desire for wicked things and give me a love for Your Word. O Lord, come into my heart, make me over and live through me. Help me to become what You want me to be. I believe that You hear my prayer and have made me a new creation. From this day on I will live for You. Thank You, dear Father. I pray in the Name of my Saviour, Jesus Christ. Amen."

If you prayed that prayer and really meant it, you are now a child of God and your sins are forgiven. You have begun a new life — old things are passed away. You have Christ living within your heart and you'll never be alone again.

I remember when my little son, Jamie, accepted the Lord, he was just five years old. He was thrilled with the idea that Christ now lived within him. Several times he came to Tammy and me to ask, "Does Jesus really live inside my heart now?" Each time we assured him that He did.

Not long afterward Jamie came through the room. His teeth were clenched together tightly, and he was attempting to talk without moving his lips. When Tammy asked what he was doing, he said — as best he could mumble — "I'm trying to keep my mouth shut so Jesus won't get out!"

That might sound amusing, but I've found that many people are very insecure about their salvation. Almost every day several genuinely troubled people call our PTL prayer line or write letters to express concern about their personal spiritual condition. Often they say, "I asked God to forgive my sins, but now I'm just not sure He did. How can I know I'm saved?"

Others say, "I'm so afraid of failing the Lord. Pray that I'll stay true and make it to the end."

Many people have a hard time understanding that becoming a Christian does not make them perfect overnight! Accepting Christ's forgiveness for your sins does not make you immune to temptation or exempt from mistakes — even sinful practices. Professing faith in God does not mean you will never again struggle with doubt.

Remember this — you are saved, not because you

feel like it, but because God's Word says you are. Feelings fluctuate with your moods and emotions, but God's Word never changes.

And if you fail — if you slip and fall — God will not turn His back on you. He understands...He cares...He wants you to make it. And He is always there to lift you up and help you begin again. As often as you ask, He will forgive.

Oh, the enemy of your soul will try to make you doubt. He'll say that you've messed up so bad you might as well quit. The Bible says he is the accuser of the brethren (see Revelation 12:10). So if you are being accused, chances are you're hearing the voice of Satan. Jesus did not come to accuse you or condemn you but to save you.

Victory over doubt and temptation

Virtually every Christian I know has gone through times of testing and struggle. All of us have struggled with making our lives conform to Christ's example and with changing our attitudes and behavior. There are times when we seem to be making progress — other times it's hard not to be overwhelmed by discouragement.

Often young Christians have said to me, "Jim, I just can't live for God — I've tried and failed so many times. Surely no one else has gone through the ordeal I'm experiencing!"

Oh, really! See if you can relate to what this believer wrote. Have you ever had any feelings like his?

"I don't understand myself at all, for I really want to do what is right, but I can't. I do what I don't want to — what I hate. I know perfectly well that what I am doing

32

is wrong, and my bad conscience proves that I agree with these laws I am breaking. But I can't help myself, because I'm no longer doing it. It is sin inside me that is stronger than I am that makes me do these evil things.

"I know that I am rotten through and through so far as my old sinful nature is concerned. No matter which way I turn I can't make myself do right. I want to but I can't. When I want to do good, I don't; and when I try not to do wrong, I do it anyway. Now if I am doing what I don't want to, it is plain where the trouble is: sin still has me in its evil grasp...So you see how it is: my new life tells me to do right, but the old nature that is still inside me loves to sin. Oh, what a terrible predicament I'm in!"

Does that sound like it could have come out of your diary? Do you suppose it must have been written by some other marginal Christian who really never had much in the first place?

Would you believe it was written by one of the greatest missionaries, apostles, and Christian teachers who ever lived — Paul! (see Romans 7:15-24, The Living Bible). That's right, even as great a Christian as Paul did not achieve instant and everlasting perfection. And how did he deal with the problem?

"Who will free me from my slavery to this deadly lower nature?" he cried. Then he answered his own question: *Thank God! It has been done by Jesus Christ our Lord. He has set me free"* (Romans 7:24, The Living Bible).

We are in God's hand

One of the most encouraging and helpful Bible stories I've ever read is found in the eighteenth chapter of Jeremiah. It is the account of how the prophet went down to the potter's house one day to watch him work. He watched with great interest as the craftsman put some clay on his wheel and shaped it into a beautiful, graceful pitcher. But just as it was almost finished, something went wrong. Perhaps there was an imperfection in the clay — an impurity that weakened the material until it could not respond to the touch of the master's hand. And the whole vessel was marred and spoiled.

But the potter did not throw the pitcher away. Instead, he kneaded the clay again in his hands, removing the impurities that had weakened and ruined the vessel. Then he made the clay into another pitcher, just the size and shape he thought best.

As Jeremiah stood there watching, the Lord spoke to him and said, *"Behold, as the clay is in the potter's hand, so are ye in mine hand"* (Jeremiah 18:6).

Isn't that tremendous? Just thinking of that makes my heart beat faster. God said we are in His hand. He wants to mold us and make us into vessels of honor. In His hands, we can become something far better than we ever thought we could be.

It may well be that as he begins to shape us, something will happen to mar the vessel we were becoming. Some impurity or imperfection may spoil the shape, the finish. But the Master Potter does not cast us aside. No, He keeps us in His hands. He kneads and works the material of our lives, taking out all the impurities and imperfections so we can be the beautiful, useful, perfect people He wants us to be.

So often I meet men and women who don't understand what God wants to do for them. They act as if they are afraid God might make them into something they don't want to be. They almost seem to think He wants something bad for them. So they resist and draw back, trying their best to get away from the hand of God.

If only we could learn that God's will for us is good.

He loves us. He wants to make us more than we are. He wants to give us more than we have. He wants to make us better than we can be on our own. He wants us to make it!

We are in His hand, and He wants to put us on His wheel to make us into what seems good to Him. But first He must take away some of the impurities and imperfections that keep us from being all He wants us to be.

So He starts removing the ugly stain and painful, abrasive stones of sin. Any form of sin, if not removed, is fatal to the soul. It corrupts the appetites, destroys character and separates man from God. It turns a person against his fellowmen, brings hate into the heart, causes inner conflicts, frustrations, torments, fears and misery. Sin is destructive. God cannot create a good vessel from clay that is contaminated by sin.

So He made a way to take away our sins. He gave His Son, the Lord Jesus Christ. *"Behold the Lamb of God, which taketh away the sin of the world"* (John 1:29). All we have to do to rid ourselves of sin is to confess it and believe and receive Christ. The Bible says, *"If we confess our sins, he is faithful and just to forgive us our sins, and to cleanse us from all unrighteousness"* (1 John 1:9).

Then He takes away the impurities of spiritual weakness. Fear, uncertainty, and lack of faith can keep you from being the strong, triumphant, victorious person God wants you to be. So He gives promise after promise to lift you up and give you confidence and power.

"Behold, I give unto you power...over all the power of the enemy: and nothing shall by any means hurt you" (Luke 10:19).

"Fear thou not; for I am with thee: be not dismayed;

for I am thy God: I will strengthen thee; yea, I will help thee" (Isaiah 41:10). *"My grace is sufficient for thee"* (2 Corinthians 12:9). *"Greater is he that is in you, than he that is in the world"* (1 John 4:4). *"All things are possible to him that believeth"* (Mark 9:23).

Aren't you glad you're in His hand? Isn't it wonderful to know that God wants you to be strong and victorious? You don't have to be weak and helpless and fearful. You can make it.

Chapter Three
How To Guarantee Success

As a child of God, you ought to live in victory. Christianity is a winning way of life. God intends for you to be successful in every part of your living.

Unfortunately, many Christians do not realize this. They somehow have been conditioned to accept — indeed, to expect — failure. Surrounded by an atmosphere of negativism and self-pity, they resign themselves to being second or third class citizens, inferior, end of the line.

This attitude is not Scriptural. This lifestyle is not Christian.

God is not defeated. He is not a failure. His resources are not limited.

Why, then, should His children, the citizens of His kingdom, live in defeat, failure, and want?

God's will for you is good. He has declared in His Word, *"Beloved, I wish above all things that thou mayest prosper and be in health, even as thy soul prospereth"* (3 John 2). He *expects* you to be successful. He has cancelled the claim of sin and death on your life and placed all the power and resources of heaven at your disposal.

So it's not God's fault if you're not successful!

Don't blame God for your failure — He's given you all you need to be a winner. Through His love, His blessings, His Word — in every conceivable way — He constantly assures you that you can make it.

The devil can't defeat you. He absolutely cannot overwhelm any child of God who knows and uses his rights and privileges as a born-again believer. I'm convinced fearful people often attribute more power to Satan than he really has. They make him stronger than he is. And that's fine with him! He is a liar and a deceiver, and if he can bluff Christians into thinking they are defeated and helpless, he will.

So if God doesn't keep us from success, and the devil can't — why aren't more Christians successful?

The answer is obvious — they defeat themselves!

That's right — you are responsible for your own success or failure. Don't misunderstand me, I'm not preaching humanism. I'm not saying man controls his own destiny, separate and independent of all other forces in the universe. I recognize and believe that without God we can do nothing — that in Him we live, and move, and have our being (Acts 17:28).

But God has already given us the keys to victory. And He has defeated our foe, Satan, the enemy of our soul. That's why I say the responsibility for our success now rests with us. God has already done all He can do for us until we begin to take action on our own!

Over the years, God has taught me some valuable lessons about how to succeed. One thing I've learned is that being successful doesn't mean one will never have a challenge or a problem. Success has to do with how you handle those challenges!

Being successful doesn't mean you'll knock a home run every time you go up to bat. Babe Ruth, the great American sports hero who was known as "the home run king," was also the strikeout king! But striking out didn't defeat him. The next time he went to bat he was even more determined to get a hit.

I want to share with you some of the keys to success God has shown me. There are certain principles in the Bible so powerful that putting them into practice will literally guarantee success.

Set goals for yourself

Mr. Webster's definition of success is:
*The favorable or prosperous termination of
anything attempted; the attainment of a
proposed object as wealth, position, or the like.*

In other words, if you obtain what you set out to obtain you are considered a success. Many people are not successful because they have not set any goals for themselves. They don't know where they are going so they never know if they have arrived. Setting a goal and then working until you reach that goal produces success.

People who conduct success motivation seminars have refined Webster's definition. They say, "Success is the *progressive* attainment of desired goals." You see, reaching one goal and retiring may not be very great success. You should move from one goal to another... and then on to another.

The apostle Paul, one of the most successful Christians who ever lived, said, *"This one thing I do, forgetting those things which are behind, and reaching forth unto those things which are before, I press toward the mark for the prize of the high calling of God in Christ Jesus"* (Philippians 3:13).

If you are going to be a successful person, you have to forget the past. Its accomplishments and achievements won't help you now. Neither can the mistakes and failures of yesterday keep you from reaching today's goal. The devil would like you to remember your past sins, but you must leave them under the blood of Christ.

When I was a little boy, my pet dog Lucky was hit by a car. He had been my constant companion for 12 years, and his death was almost more than I could stand. I had a funeral for Lucky and buried him. I even found an old, battered tombstone behind the cemetery to mark his grave.

But I couldn't get over my pet's death. I kept on grieving for Lucky. I don't know why, but a few days later I decided to dig him up. And I did! All I can say is *I should have left him buried!*

There may be some things in your past that ought to be left buried. Some people have a little "sin box" they open up every now and then to play with the sins of the past — to remember them and agonize over them. And as long as they do that it's almost impossible for them to move toward their goals. Forget the past. Leave your sins buried beneath the blood of Christ. Like Paul, reach *"forth unto those things which are before."*

Define your goals. Get them clearly in mind — better still, write them down! You must have goals if you're going to be successful.

You need goals for your spiritual life. I had a goal to be filled with the Holy Spirit before I entered Bible school. I was brought up in a Pentecostal church and knew all about the Baptism, but I had not experienced it in my own life. I said, "God, fill me before I enter Bible school." And He did. About 12 hours before classes were to begin on the first day of school, God filled me with the Holy Ghost. That was the attainment of a spiritual goal in my life.

The dictionary defines the word "goal" as *"the place at which a race or journey is to end; the final purpose or aim that is desired, and that which a person aims to reach or obtain."*

With that in mind, each of us should have a goal to make heaven our final home. That is where this race and this journey called life is going to end. I choose to have my goal end in heaven! That will be the ultimate success.

You need goals for your family. Couples starting out should have a goal that they will stay married! Too many people today — even Christians — are failing in their marriages. Divorce is defeating them. Also, parents should have goals for their children — especially that their children should grow up knowing and loving God.

You should have goals for your health — that you are going to be well. Reaching that goal means working out a sensible plan for daily living — a plan that includes proper diet, exercise, and rest.

You need goals for your financial life. I firmly believe every family should have a budget — a *written* budget that is followed. In today's economic climate there is little room for error. Financial success demands careful planning and prudent use of your income. So follow a budget. And remember that the single most important item on your budget is your tithe! The first 10 percent of your income belongs to the Lord. If you are faithful to give the firstfruits of your income to God, He has promised to *"open you the windows of heaven, and pour you out a blessing, that there shall not be room enough to receive it"* (Malachi 3:10).

Take time to establish your goals. Make a list of your goals for this year, five years from now — perhaps even longer. Then start moving toward those goals. Don't let anybody steal your dreams and turn you away from your goals. Use the problems you face as stepping-stones to victory.

In the game of ice hockey there is one player called the goal keeper or goalie. From the name, you might think his job is to help you get to the goal. In reality, it's just the opposite. His function is to defend his team's goal and keep you from scoring. Every time you shoot for the goal, he tries to block you or knock the puck away!

41

The devil has lots of "goalies" to keep you from the goal. They may try to steer you away from the right path and say, "Go ahead and try it; everybody else is doing it." Or they might say, "Don't try so hard — you're taking on too much. Back off a little; there's plenty of time!"

These goalies will keep you from being what God wants you to be if you let them. Make sure you surround yourself with teammates who are pressing toward the same goals you are. And don't ever lose sight of your goals.

Develop and maintain a positive attitude

In recent years there has been some controversy over the concept of "positive confession" — of claiming the promises of God's Word for the needs of life even before the desired blessing becomes a reality. Critics were concerned over what they saw as excesses that could lead to error. Enthusiasts charged that opponents were simply displaying a lack of faith.

Without getting involved in that discussion, let me just say that the Bible teaches that we should have a positive attitude, and that it is a vital foundation stone for success. The Word of God is full of teachings that stress the benefits of positive, faith-filled thinking.

Some of my favorite verses are about this theme. Proverbs 23:7 says, *"For as he thinketh in his heart, so is he."* Matthew 12:34 declares, *"For out of the abundance of the heart the mouth speaketh."* And Philippians 4:13 says, *"I can do all things through Christ which strengtheneth me."*

I know this — if I begin to think negatively and talk negatively, everything in my whole world begins to go wrong. But as soon as I realize what I'm doing and get a hold of myself, I can turn things around by changing my attitude! *Literally*. If I go to God's Word and read His promises — if I strengthen my faith with the positive truths of the Bible, it's amazing how quickly circumstances fall into line with my attitude, thinking, and positive confession!

I heard about a grandfather who was taking a nap one day and the children decided to play a trick on him. They got some Limburger cheese and put the smelly stuff in his mustache. Grandpa woke up in a big hurry and said, "This room stinks!" He ran outside and took a deep breath, then declared, "The whole world stinks!"

There are many people just like that today who go around saying that everything is rotten. And when they say it and look for rottenness, they find it. Wherever they go they carry rottenness with them. Their very attitude spoils their world just like vinegar sours fresh milk.

Sometimes I think the news media programs our whole nation for failure and defeat. Millions of Americans start off the day with the morning newspaper, which is filled from top to bottom with bad news — murder, rape, robbery, dire predictions...page after page of sadness and sorrow, gloom and doom. They tune in the radio news on the way to work and hear more of the same. They work all day around other negatively-programmed people who talk about rumors that the company is going broke and everybody is going to get laid off, and they get home in time to eat supper and worry about how grocery prices are going up. Then they watch the evening news on television to see full-color, close-up pictures of car wreck victims and war scenes. After all that, it's time to go to bed and try to rest!

No wonder there is so much negativism in the

world. Have you ever noticed how everyday conversation is hardly ever positive? We talk about red lights, not green lights. The milk bottle is always half empty, not half full. And when people gossip, they always talk about bad things — hurtful things. Have you ever heard a bunch of gossips sit around and see how many good things they could think of to say about people?

It irks me to hear people say they don't go to church because there's a hypocrite there. Why don't they acknowledge all the good people there — the godly, upstanding, loving people? That makes about as much sense as saying they will never eat another apple for the rest of their lives because they once found a worm in one. Why would anyone want to spend his whole life looking for worms instead of enjoying apples?

We can change our world with a positive mental attitude. That's why I say that a positive attitude is one of the guarantees of success.

I heard about a shoe company that sent a salesman to open a new territory in Africa. After just one day he cabled the home office: "Send me a ticket to get out of here — they don't wear shoes in this place."

The company was determined to open that section of Africa so they sent their top salesman to see what he could do. In a matter of hours after his arrival, he, too, cabled the home office. But his wire said, "Send all the shoes you can spare. This is the best market I have ever seen. NOBODY has any shoes."

Be sure your attitude is positive. How can you do that? Watch what you say. I'm sure you've heard the old axiom that if you can't say something good about a person, don't say anything at all. That's good advice! But I'd encourage you to carry it even further — if you can't say something good, something positive about *anything,* it's better to say nothing.

And my second suggestion is, don't listen to others saying bad things. If your friends are negative thinkers and negative talkers, they will ultimately influence you to be negative too. If you really want to make it — if you're serious about wanting to be successful — you may have to find some new friends!

Surround yourself with positive people. I like to be around people with faith. It does me good to have people around me saying, "Jim, we can make it. We're conquerors through Christ. We're winners!" And if you want to keep a positive attitude, associate with people who have wisdom, who have good advice and good words to speak.

Last, but not least, keep feeding your mind and spirit on the Word of God. Remember, if you want to reap a positive harvest, you must sow positive seeds. As computer technicians have learned, you get back what you put in — "garbage in, garbage out!"

The psalmist said, *"Thy word have I hid in mine heart, that I might not sin against thee"* (Psalm 119:11). Fill your mind with God's Word. Meditate on the scriptures that encourage and build you up. Memorize verses that will help you in times of temptation and trouble.

So many people rely on experiential Christianity instead of the basic fundamentals of the Word of God. That's why the devil can come against them and destroy their positive attitude so easily. Satan always attacks when we're at our lowest ebb — when we're feeling tired, weak, or discouraged. Remember how he tempted Jesus in the wilderness after the Lord had fasted forty days. Each time the tempter came to Him, Jesus answered from the Word of God. The Word gave Him power to defeat Satan. And it will do the same for you.

Jesus said to His disciples — and to you and me —

"For verily I say unto you, That whosoever shall say unto this mountain, Be thou removed, and be thou cast into the sea; and shall not doubt in his heart, but shall believe that those things which he saith shall come to pass; he shall have whatsoever he saith. Therefore I say unto you, What things soever ye desire, when ye pray, believe that ye receive them, and ye shall have them" (Mark 11:23, 24).

You can have victory in Jesus Christ.

You can speak faith and change your life.

With a positive attitude, you can make it.

Be willing to go the second mile

Shortly after Jesus began His earthly ministry, He went up on a hillside overlooking the Sea of Galilee and began to teach the multitude that gathered about Him. This discourse, known as the Sermon on the Mount, is packed full of powerful, important teachings.

One of these statements caught my attention in a special way one day. Jesus said, *"And whosoever shall compel thee to go a mile, go with him twain"* (Matthew 5:41).

In Jesus' day, the armies of Rome controlled much of the known world, and Roman occupation forces kept the Jewish people in subjection. According to their law, a soldier could stop any person and have him carry his military pack or other burden for a distance of one mile. Then another person could be conscripted and the first person let go. An example of this practice happened on the day of Jesus' crucifixion, when Simon of Cyrene was forced to carry the cross of Calvary.

As He taught the people, Jesus said, "If someone forces you to go a mile with him, go two miles instead." As I read this, I sensed that it was an important truth for you and me — a key to Christian success.

46

I checked to see what Webster's Dictionary had to say about "second mile," but I couldn't find any reference at all. I tried a big Bible dictionary — it wasn't there either. After checking several other reference works and finding nothing, I came up with my own definition. Being a second miler is "rendering more and better service than one is paid or asked for."

Jesus was saying, "If you want to be successful, if you want to make it — give more than you have to, do more than is required, be better than you're expected to be."

That's the opposite of what the modern generation tries to do. Today's labor force wants to get to work late and leave early — they want more money for less work. It's no wonder the quality of some American products has declined, with workers saying, "That's good enough — it'll probably get by."

It's really no surprise to read about large companies that are losing money — entire chains of department stores closing down. I've gone shopping in some of these stores and the salesclerks made me feel like they were doing me a favor to wait on me — that's if I could even find a salesperson at all.

Some time ago I was buying a new car, and the model I wanted was not in stock and had to be ordered. The dealer told me when the car should arrive. On the day my car was supposed to be ready, I eagerly waited for the salesman to call and tell me to come pick it up. But he didn't call. I didn't hear from him the next day either. So I called to ask when I could expect the car to be in.

I was shocked at how rudely I was treated! The salesman's attitude and tone of voice let me know he wished I wouldn't bother him. He told me my car wasn't there and he didn't know when it would be. He seemed

47

reluctant to even call and check on it for me.

Do you know what I did? I cancelled my order for the car. I didn't need it that bad. And besides, I knew there were plenty of other places I could buy a car...from people who would be more appreciative of my business.

Just a few weeks later I saw in the paper that this car dealership went out of business. All I can say is that if they treated all their customers the way they treated me, they deserved to go under.

You can be successful...you can make it, even in the more austere economic conditions of our times. But you must be willing to go the second mile — to give more, do more, be more than is expected of you. Success seldom goes to shirkers and corner cutters.

Do the best job you can for your employer. Be willing to get there a little early or stay a bit late. Find a way to do it better, faster, or with less expense. It won't be long before your efforts will be noticed and you'll be rewarded or promoted!

Maybe you're saying, "Jim, you just don't know my boss. He's the meanest, most stingy man in the world. If I do more, he'll just expect more. I could kill myself for him and it wouldn't do any good."

Well, let me tell you something. Go the second mile anyway. Why? Because the source of your blessings is not your employer. Your source is God. The person or company that writes your check is just an instrument, a channel God uses. And if they refuse to reward your better work, God will send your blessing from some other source. You'll get moved to some other department, or some other company will hire you, or God will find some totally unexpected way to bless you.

God's Word is true. And the Bible says, *"Give, and it shall be given unto you; good measure, pressed down, and shaken together, and running over, shall men give into your bosom. For with the same measure that ye mete withal it shall be measured to you again"* (Luke 6:38).

Did you get that? If you give good measure, you're going to get good measure! But if you try to cheat and gyp others, you're only hurting yourself.

One of the most exciting men I've ever met is Charlie Jones. They call him "Mr. Tremendous" because he likes that word so much and uses it all the time. He simply bursts with enthusiasm and positive energy and he can excite a crowd like no man I have ever heard. He tells a story that illustrates why it's important to be a second miler and how doing your best always pays off.

It seems a young man married a nice girl, the daughter of a very well-to-do businessman. The father-in-law came to his daughter's new husband and said, "Son, I want to help you kids get started. I know you are a building contractor, so I want to give you a job. I'd like you to build a house for me."

Now, the son-in-law may have been expecting something besides a job from his wife's father, I don't know. But he agreed to build the house.

"There's just one thing," said the father-in-law. "I want this house to be the best, the finest house you can possibly build. I want you to use the best materials you can find and hire the best craftsmen to do the work. Money is no object, so don't hold back. I'll pay whatever it costs...and there will be a nice profit in the job for you. But I want you to build me a palace — I mean, I want it to be TREMENDOUS!"

So the son-in-law started building. But along the way he got greedy. He thought, "This old man's got more money than he knows what to do with, so I might as well get a little of it. I can cut back on some of the expensive materials in this house and buy cheaper stuff. I can keep the difference and he'll never know. And I can hire cheaper labor to do the work — it'll be good enough. He'll probably never even notice. And if he does, what's he going to do about it? After all, I am his daughter's husband. He'd never do anything that would hurt her."

So he built the house as cheap as he could. He used shoddy material and poor workmanship. He threw a house together that — as "Tremendous" Jones says — wouldn't last through two gale winds. It was a poor house — but he made a tremendous profit on it.

When the house was finished, the father-in-law said, "Did you build it good?"

"Oh, yes, I did a good job."

"Did you use the best materials — did you make it a real palace?"

"Yes, sir, I did."

"All right, then, here's the key to your new home! This house is my gift to you and my daughter. That's why I insisted that it be the very best. You have just built your own house!"

The young man cheated himself! That's what happens if you don't do your best and go the second mile. If you cheat at school, at work, if you cheat your friends, you're really only hurting yourself. You may get by for a day, or even a year, but you will lose in the end.

When you go the extra mile and give of yourself, you actually are planting good seeds in your own garden. And you will harvest a bountiful crop — a blessing that will help you make it and be truly successful.

Let love be your greatest success

The single most important law of success is love!

You can have all the other qualities you need. You can have all the talent and natural ability in the world. You can have all the capital and ideas and know all the right people. But unless you have love, you are doomed to failure before you start. Love is vital to any endeavor...in every part of your life.

Successful people are loving people. Those who make it are those who love.

God is love. His Spirit is love. Faith works by love (see 1 John 4:8; Galatians 5:22; Galatians 5:6).

We are to love God. Deep down, I suppose, every person realizes this is true. And because of His greatness, His power and majesty, His love, most individuals find it is not too difficult to feel love for God.

It's the second part of the commandment — loving our neighbors as ourselves — that trips most of us up. How often we make excuses for not loving others. "I could love her if she hadn't said that." Or, "I could love him if he wouldn't act that way." Or, "How can I love him when he did that to me?"

But Paul, writing about love to the believers at Corinth, insisted, *"It does not hold grudges and will hardly even notice when others do it wrong"* (1 Corinthians 13:5, The Living Bible).

God's Word teaches that we are to love unconditionally. When someone makes a mistake we are still to love. When your wife isn't the way you want her to be, you still are to love her. When your husband doesn't act the way he is supposed to, you still must love him.

We have let our "disposable" way of living influence our attitude toward people. We're so accustomed to using disposable cups, handkerchiefs, plates, napkins, clothes, etc., and then throwing them away that we're starting to treat people in the same manner. When people outlive their usefulness, or make a mistake, or become an embarrassment — we just toss them out.

I tell you, we can't just wad people up like a dirty Kleenex and throw them away!

In the last few years I have seen several fellow ministers "hit the dust," as they say in western movies. Some of the greatest soul-winning evangelists of this generation are not even preaching today. They slipped. They made a mistake. They hurt others and themselves.

So what happened? Suddenly no one knew them. Nobody wanted to be seen with them. Like the beaten and robbed traveler in the Good Samaritan story, everybody went around him and hurried on their way without looking back, even the Priest and Levite! Have you ever seen that happen? Someone once said that the ministry is the only brotherhood where they shoot their own wounded! And they might have added that if anyone else tries to help the wounded, he gets shot too!

But that's not right! When a brother falls he doesn't cease to be a brother. I have an obligation to go out and pick him up and bring him back to fellowship.

It's a risky business to love, but if we are going to win our generation for Christ we are going to have to love.

Divorce is a major problem today. It not only has devastated the non-Christian homes in America, but has crushed and broken thousands of Christian families as well. The divorced people I have talked with tell me that one of the worst parts of divorce is the rejection they feel from former friends and associates.

I'm not in favor of divorce — I hate it. But how can we close our eyes and say there is not such a thing as divorce today? We are going to have to learn to deal with it and let God be the judge. We are going to have to love these people who are hurting, who are scared, who are emotionally battered. God help us to see that when these people come to church for help, they need to be loved and healed, not kicked again.

I'm not defending divorce — I'm just endorsing love! It's time we become doers of the Word and not just hearers. If you don't love the Body of Christ, it doesn't matter how religious you are, how much money you give, whether or not you speak in tongues, or how much you shout. John wrote, *"We know that we have passed from death unto life, because we love the brethren. He that loveth not his brother abideth in death"* (1 John 3:14).

If you don't love, you are not a Christian.

If you don't forgive others, you are not forgiven.

Maybe you're saying, "I just can't forgive them."

Well, it's your own business if you go to hell! If you want to go to hell, just keep your grudges, hate everybody, feel sorry for yourself, and live with pity demons. You'll make it straight into hell!

You say, "Jim, that's mean."

No it isn't. That's the truth, and it's the most loving thing I can tell you. For unless someone helps you see the truth that you must forgive and love, you will end up eternally separated from God, asking, "What did I do wrong?"

Jesus said, *"For if ye forgive men their trespasses, your heavenly Father will also forgive you: but if ye forgive not men their trespasses, neither will your Father forgive your trespasses"* (Matthew 6:14, 15).

Forgive. Be forgiven.

Love. Be loved.

Let Christ's forgiveness make you whole again. Let His love give you new life. And as the love of Jesus flows into you, let your love flow to others.

The best way to demonstrate your love for God — the way you can best serve Him is to love and serve others. You may think you have to build a church, help a missionary, or support the work of the Lord through different ministries. And those are all good worthy projects. But God may direct you to feed a hungry family, give them a place to stay for a few days, or provide clothes for a needy stranger. You may visit an "abandoned" grandmother in an old folks home, sit with a sick friend in the hospital, or go to share your testimony in a jail or prison.

Jesus said, *"Inasmuch as ye have done it unto one of the least of these my brethren, ye have done it unto me"* (Matthew 25:40).

The true test of the Body of Christ is how one member responds to the needs of another. *"There should be no schism in the body; but that the members should have the same care one for another. And whether one member suffer, all the members suffer with it; or one member be honoured, all the members rejoice with it"* (1 Corinthians 12:25, 26).

Don't be disturbed or upset by the dire predictions of gloom and doom you may hear about the days to come. You can make it in the closing days of time...through love.

If you stay in the Body of Christ — the fellowship of believers — there is no reason for fear. The Body of Christ is the greatest survival capsule you could hope for. As Christians, we will stand together, caring for one another, loving one another...and then Jesus will come to take us all to be with Him forever.

How to know success through God's timing

If you want to be successful, you have to understand timing — God's timing.

The first seven verses of Ecclesiastes 3 is a catalogue of times. Solomon declared, *"To every thing there is a season, and a time to every purpose under the heaven: a time to be born, and a time to die..."* And he goes on to list more than a dozen other examples.

One of the chief causes of failure is improper timing — either moving too late after the doors of opportunity have closed or getting ahead of God's plan and moving before we're ready. The problem is that we cannot see the whole scope of God's plan — we see only a short span immediately around us. We don't even know about tomorrow. But God sees the end from the beginning. He alone knows when we should take action. And only as we stay in contact with Him can we avoid making eternal mistakes.

At one of Mexico's most famous resorts, tourists watch as divers climb to the top of high cliffs overlooking a tidal cove. Looking like a speck on the huge boulder at the top, the diver assumes a graceful pose, hesitating until a precise split-second instant arrives. Then he swoops out, and in a classic swan position, he hurtles past the jagged rocks of the cliff, down toward...more jagged rocks!

For at the moment the diver leaps into the air, the tide is out. The natural pool toward which his body plummets appears to have only a few inches of water in it. Down, down, down he dives, arms outstretched like wings, legs extended, back arched, seemingly oblivious to the certain disaster below.

But as he falls...the tide comes in. And just as his

hands touch the water, the waves surge under him at their highest level and he slips safely into their depths!

What courage it must take to leap off the cliff when there is no water in the pool below. Yet, if the diver waited until it looked safe to make his jump, by the time he reached the bottom the tide would be out again and his body would be smashed on the rocks below.

There have been many times when God has told me to jump...and I hesitated because conditions didn't seem right to me. "Lord, are you sure? I'd better wait until I have more experience, more money, more supporters, less obligations. I'm just not ready."

A few times the Lord has given me a nudge and I found myself falling over the edge, kicking and screaming, certain that I would be smashed on the rocks. But when I got there, the cushioning waves were waiting to receive me.

There were other times — although I don't especially like to remember them — when I insisted on waiting until I thought the time was right. I started off fine. I even looked pretty good going down. But when I arrived at the bottom, the tide was out! Only the mercy of God kept me from being destroyed on the rocks. And I got my nose scraped painfully enough as it was!

Have you ever got out of God's timing by waiting too long to act? Have you ever missed the boat? Do you know what it's like to finally get up the nerve to go through the door of opportunity, only to find it was closed and locked by the time you finally got there?

That's what happens when we wait too long to move and miss God's timing.

But perhaps even more often we try to move too fast and get ahead of God. The Lord begins to show us something we are to do in the future. Immediately we get up and start for the door, and God has to say, "Just wait until it's time — don't get impatient."

When Tammy bakes a cake, the whole family gathers in the kitchen and gets ready to eat it before she even takes it out of the oven. The children keep saying, "Isn't it done yet? Take it out, Momma. It's probably ready right now."

Sometimes Tammy has to run us out of the kitchen. "I don't even want you all in here until it's done. And don't touch the oven as you go by or you'll cause the cake to fall and ruin it."

You can imagine how hard it is for her to get that cake cooled and iced before the kids and I get into it. How we enjoy that fresh, moist cake!

But if Tammy let us have our way and we took the cake out of the oven before it was ready, all we'd get is a mushy, sticky mess!

Suppose a farmer planted his seed, then went back the next day and dug them up to see if the crop was ready yet? Wouldn't that be foolish? Yet, that's how we act sometimes when God tells us we need to wait.

God does not get in a hurry. He is not anxious. His timing is always right — never too early, never too late.

Beware of voices of haste. When someone comes to you and says, "Sign on the dotted line right now — you can't wait or it will be too late," you had better watch out. Someone is trying to put something over on you. God doesn't have to say, "Panic time!" He will open the door when it is time, and not one minute sooner.

One day I announced on television that we were going into Latin America with PTL. I introduced the Spanish-speaking minister we would be working with and outlined a rather ambitious missionary support program.

Several of my friends probably though I was leaping before I looked — taking off on the spur of the moment. But that wasn't the case at all.

Some 20 years before God had spoken to Tammy and me about Latin America and placed a real burden on our hearts for Spanish-speaking people. At first we thought God was calling us to be missionaries, and we began making plans to go. We even went out and sought the support of several churches because we were willing — even eager — to go. Then, in a sudden and dramatic way, God closed the door.

We were almost embarrassed not to go because so many friends had promised to help support us on the mission field. But God said, "No."

We ended up in evangelistic work, then pioneering Christian television. And at times we said, "Lord, were we mistaken when we thought You were calling us to Latin America?" But our love for Spanish-speaking people stayed with us, and the burden we felt to reach them with the Gospel did not let up.

Almost 20 years went by. Then God said, "Now is the time to reach Latin America." But now we were not going personally to one small area on the Amazon, preaching to one tribe here, a village there. Through television, we were to take the Gospel to whole countries. Now, millions of people see the Spanish version of PTL every week. Moving in God's time, we are reaching more people in Latin America than probably any group in the history of world evangelism.

If Tammy and I had rushed on down to be missionaries on the Amazon, there might never have been a PTL ministry. Thank God we were willing to wait on the Lord!

Be sensitive to the leading of God's Holy Spirit in your life. Let Him guide you, lead you, prompt you. Depend on God to show you His time to move, His time to wait.

In your planning, give God a chance to say, "No, stop, wait." Every time I begin a project I say, "Lord, I'm convinced this is what You want me to do. But if I'm mistaken, stop me. Close all the doors." Delays, zoning problems, financial difficulties, and other situations can all be used of God to slow or stop what we're doing. I've learned not to let myself be irritated by them. I know God will make a way to get the job done when the timing is right.

To be successful, build your plans around God's plan for your life. Be sure you understand what you are to do. Then let God direct you to take each step on His time schedule.

When you are moving according to God's timing, nothing can stop you and...*you can make it!*

Success through agreement

Another absolutely essential key to success is the power of agreement. If you are to be successful in your home, your business, you church, there must be unity, harmony, *agreement.*

The Old Testament prophet Amos asked, *"Can two walk together, except they be agreed?"* (Amos 3:3). The implication is pretty obvious. If two people are not in agreement, they won't walk together very long. There will come a parting of the ways. First, disagreement causes both individuals to look inward and away from their common goal. Then they begin focusing on the area of contention instead of the things they agree on.

A business with partners who do not agree is almost sure to fail. There must be one person who can make the final decision...and an agreement that his decision will stand. Otherwise there will be a dividing and a separation that will destroy the business.

Jesus said, *"Every kingdom divided against itself is brought to desolation; and every city or house divided against itself shall not stand"* (Matthew 12:25). Division will bring destruction.

When a husband has one blueprint for life and the wife another, they cannot build a stable marriage. There must be agreement. Without it, there will soon come a parting of the ways. When there is a lack of unity between Mom and Dad, the kids pick it up right away too. And even a four-year-old can learn how to manipulate his parents and work one against the other!

When the household is divided with one parent against the other and one parent siding with the kids, strife and misery is certain. And unless there is a change — unless agreement is restored through reconciliation — divorce and a broken home will result.

But it doesn't have to be that way. There can be agreement in your home, your business, your church, your personal life. And that agreement will produce and release a power that helps guarantee success.

Take a look at what Solomon said would happen if just two people agreed together — *"Two can accomplish more than twice as much as one, for the results can be much better. If one falls, the other pulls him up; but if a man falls when he is alone, he's in trouble. Also, on a cold night, two under the same blanket gain warmth from each other, but how can one be warm alone? And one standing alone can be attacked and defeated, but two can stand back-to-back and conquer"* (Ecclesiastes 4:9-12, The Living Bible).

The power of agreement is awesome. I'm thinking of a particular event in Church history which has turned the world upside down. It has changed the face of Christianity and set the Church on fire. This event marked the empowering of the Church to go forward under the anointing of the Holy Spirit. Of course, I'm speaking of Pentecost.

The Bible says, *"And when the day of Pentecost was fully come, they were all with one accord in one place"* (Acts 2:1, emphasis added).

If any church wants to have the power to turn the world upside down to win souls for Christ, the people must come together and be in one accord. There must be agreement if there is to be power!

Do you want miracles in your home? Do you want God's blessings on your business? Do you want spiritual power? Do you want to be successful?

You must learn the power of agreement. Your marriage partner and your children must get in agreement. Your business associates or partners must be in harmony. Your church members must work together in unity. Standing firm together in love and agreement, you can face just about anything. You can win. You can make it!

For almost two decades my personal key verse has been Matthew 18:19: *"If two of you shall agree on earth as touching any thing that they shall ask, it shall be done for them of my Father which is in heaven."*

Almost every day I'm on television, I ask my audience to agree with me in prayer for our various ministries around the world — for my family, my staff, for those who are viewing the program who need salvation, healing, or the answer to some other need. It's amazing how God has honored His Word and answered those prayers of agreement time after time. A few years ago I compiled an entire book of testimonies of answered prayer.

"If two of you shall agree..." Write it down.

Practice it! See what will happen when you join hands with someone and say, "I agree with you in the Name of Jesus."

Let's you and I agree together for victory in our lives...and for the evangelization of the whole world.

When we agree together and harness this great spiritual force, we cannot fail. We will be successful. We can make it!

Chapter Four

The Shortest Route Out Of The Valley

Trouble.

Sooner or later it comes to everybody. I'm sure you've often heard the familiar saying, "Into each life some rain must fall." And it's true.

Rain is not too difficult to accept as long as it's only spoiling picnics or parades — we can always remind ourselves that the thirsty earth needs a drink, that farmers are glad for it, and that "April showers bring May flowers." But when the rain is coming down in torrents for the umpteenth day, the rivers are flooding, and your house and all you own in the world are floating away — it's hard to look at rain philosophically.

But like it or not, trouble comes. You might as well know and accept that right now. No amount of positive thinking or "faith talking" is going to change that.

Perhaps you're thinking, "But that's a negative outlook. That's fatalistic!"

No it isn't — it's simply realistic. No less an authority than Jesus Christ declared, *"In the world ye shall have tribulation"* (John 16:33). Notice that He didn't say we *might* have or *could* have tribulation — He said *shall* have. That means, *for sure!*

If you haven't already discovered the inevitability of trouble — you will. That's the bad news. The good news is that, with God's help, you can make it through whatever trouble may come.

In the very same verse Jesus said we'd have tribulation, He went on to say — *"But be of good cheer; I have overcome the world."*

63

I am convinced that many Christians are not very realistic about trouble. In fact, I've seen new converts almost lose their faith because they'd been led to believe that all their troubles would be over when they gave their hearts to God. They expected life to be one continuous mountaintop experience — they weren't prepared for the valley.

I've also heard mistaken and misinformed Christians talking about some fellow believer who was going through real trouble and tribulation. "There must be something wrong in her life or those bad things wouldn't be happening." Or, "He'd better get back to the Lord — God must be trying to teach him something."

What anguish those critical people must suffer when troubles come to them...when they find themselves in a valley experience. They have to try to keep it a secret from their friends or else admit that something is wrong in their life and they need to get back to God! So right when they need love and support the most, they isolate themselves and suffer in solitude and silence.

The real test for a person's Christian experience is not whether he has trouble or not — but how he deals with trouble when it comes.

How do you handle trouble?

Have you ever watched people when they were beset with trials, testings, problems, hardships — when they were in trouble? Have you observed the paths they take to try and get out of the valley?

Some become bitter and rebellious against God. "Why me?" they demand. "What did I do to deserve this? I try to live right, to serve God — I never hurt anybody. What good does it do to have faith and go to church if this is what happens?"

Others choose to ignore trouble — to pretend it doesn't exist. They say, "If I act like it's not there, maybe it'll go away."

Someone else may decide to just endure trouble. "I'll hold on if it kills me. Perhaps my suffering will glorify God. I'll just take it as long as I can."

But self-pity, self-deception, and self-imposed endurance are all roads that lead deeper into trouble, farther into the valley. They are sure routes to failure... perhaps even destruction.

The shortest route out of the valley of trouble is the praise route!

That's right — I said praise. The Christian way to handle trouble is to praise God *in* it and *for* it!

"But that's crazy!," I hear you say. And from a natural, human point of view, it is. But praise is one hundred percent scriptural — a totally biblical "secret weapon" Christians can use to win over trouble.

Merlin Carothers has been my guest on Christian television programs several times. He is the author of a series of enormously successful books on praise. He points out that if we believe that all things work together for good to them that love God, then we can be thankful for everything that comes along. Paul the apostle wrote that it is God's will for us to give thanks *"in every thing"* (1 Thessalonians 5:18) and to give thanks *"always for all things"* (Ephesians 5:20).

To be honest, I had trouble with this concept at first. It just didn't make sense to me to praise God and give thanks *for* trouble. I could kind of understand praising God when I was *in* trouble, but when I was hurting, or broke, or grief-stricken, how could I honestly give thanks for those things?

The Lord had to be patient with me. I tried all the

other paths and roads in the valley. But after many personal experiences, I began to see that feeling sorry for myself didn't make trouble go away.

Pretending my trouble wasn't there didn't get me out of the valley. No matter how loud I shouted that everything was fine and trouble was just a figment of imagination, when I quieted down that "imagination" knocked the props out from under me.

Keeping a stiff upper lip and being determined to endure my troubles didn't work either. I got saddled with some problems that were too big to carry, no matter how I strained. Sooner or later they wore me down.

So when all else failed, I decided to read the directions! I went to God's Word. Sure enough, everywhere I looked the Bible was teaching about praising and giving thanks to God. So I began to try it.

I wish I could report that I praised God and immediately all my problems were solved, my bills were paid, trouble vanished, and I floated to the top of the highest mountain and just stayed there forever. It would really be a dramatic story.

But that's not what happened. Sometimes I praised God and gave thanks in and for trouble — and it seemed to get worse! But I kept on trying to praise God. And one day I noticed that something was happening to me. I was calmer. I felt more assured. The awful fear I had lived with so often wasn't eating at my guts.

In the midst of frustrations, setbacks, disappointments — even heartaches — I found myself breathing a prayer of thanks and praise to God. And when things looked the darkest, I'd hear that inner voice of the Holy Spirit whispering to me, "Keep going, Jim, you can make it!"

Praise produces power

I discovered that praising God released power into my life to make it through the darkest night and the most trying trouble.

Carothers, in his book, *Walking and Leaping*, acknowledges that many people find it difficult to praise and thank God *for* the very situation which is causing them so much grief, bitterness, or depair. "It seems impossible that this act of blind, grit-your-teeth-and-do-it obedience could be responsible for miracles, but the act of praising does two things simultaneously: it softens the heart, and it enables the divine machinery to be set into motion on our behalf, machinery that is awesomely powerful, just waiting for the deep change of heart true praise invariably produces."

The weapon of praise

One of the most exciting accounts of the power of praise is found in the Old Testament, in 2 Chronicles 20. It's the story of a great battle that was won without God's people even having to fight. All they did was praise the Lord.

Jehoshaphat was king of Judah, and his people were in terrible trouble. Three great armies had gathered against them and threatened to totally wipe them out. Jehoshaphat knew he didn't stand a chance against the superior equipment and forces of the Moabites, the Ammonites, and the Meunites.

"O God," he prayed. *"We have no might to stand against this great company that is coming against us. We do not know what to do, but our eyes are upon you"* (see 2 Chronicles 20:12).

As Jehoshaphat and the people waited before the Lord in urgent prayer, God spoke to them through His

67

prophet. *"Don't be afraid or upset, for the battle is not yours, but God's. You don't even have to fight in this battle. Just go out before them, stand still and see the deliverance of the Lord"* (see 20:15, 17).

And that's exactly the way it happened. The next morning Jehoshaphat lined up his little army and told them what to do. He picked out the best singers, and put them at the front. Then he had them start marching out toward the three huge enemy armies, singing and praising the beauty of holiness.

Imagine how confusing this must have been to the captains of the enemy armies. There they were, just ready to swoop down on the little army of Judah and utterly destroy them. But instead of fleeing in terror, Jehoshaphat's troops came out and stood still right in front of the battlefield. And those cocky little runts were even singing and celebrating!

This wasn't how things were supposed to go at all. Watch out. It must be some kind of trick. Maybe some of our allies have joined them. So let's beat them to the punch — attack! attack! Every man for himself!

The Bible says, *"When they began to sing and to praise, the Lord set ambushments against the children of Ammon, Moab, and mount Seir, which were come against Judah; and they were smitten"* (2 Chronicles 20:22).

The armies of Ammon and Moab, in their confusion, attacked the Meunites and slaughtered them. Above the sound of battle they heard a song of praise to God. And they kept on fighting — literally killing and destroying each other.

When the army of Judah marched out later to see the multitude of soldiers — *"behold, they were dead bodies fallen to the earth, and none escaped"* (20:24).

Jehoshaphat and his people came and found an

abundance of riches and precious jewels on the bodies of the soldiers — more than they could gather up and carry away in three days. Not only had God delivered them from death and captivity, He blessed them with great wealth and riches at the same time.

There is tremendous power in praise. The prayer of praise releases more of God's power than any petition. Why? Psalm 22:3 says that God *"inhabitest the praises of Israel."* He actually lives and dwells in our praises. No wonder God's power is so near when we praise Him.

That's why you can make it...through praise. You can make it because God lives in your praise and goes out and fights your battles for you. No trouble can stand before Him — He cannot be defeated...and neither can you. Because you can say with the psalmist, *"The Lord is on my side"* (Psalm 118:6).

Praising God when things go wrong does not mean we approve of evil — it simply is acknowledging that God is at work in everything that happens. Praise is based on our acceptance of the present as part of God's plan for our life — as an expression of His loving, perfect will for us. We praise God — not for what we expect will happen — but for what God is and where and how we are right now. It is a way to express our trust in Him.

Triumph over tribulation

One of my favorite Bible characters is Job. He certainly knew about trouble. And he is a good example of how we should handle trouble and how God takes care of those who trust Him.

Job had worked hard all his life, and was finally enjoying the fruit of his labors. He had become wealthy, with abundant harvests stored up, good land holdings, large herds of livestock, a comfortable home, a beautiful family, lots of friends.

69

Then disaster struck. Robbers swept down on some of his servants, killing them and taking away the oxen, donkeys, and burros they had been caring for. One servant escaped to bring the news to Job, who was shocked and distressed.

Job's friends tried to comfort him. Some of them may have said, "Cheer up, Job, things could be worse." Like the old joke goes, Job cheered up — and sure enough, things got worse!

A messenger came with the grim news that lightning had struck his sheep, killing all of them along with the shepherds.

Another messenger rushed in to report that robbers had stolen all Job's camels.

Then came the most devastating news of all. Job's sons and daughters had been together having dinner and a great wind blew the house down upon them. They were all killed!

Job was crushed. How much trouble could one man stand. He mourned for his children, and no doubt he couldn't understand why he had suffered such financial losses. I'm sure Job must have spent a miserable, sleepless night.

And the next morning things were even worse! Job found himself covered from head to toe with boils — painful, inflamed, infected, angry red swellings. If you've every had just one boil, you can imagine how Job must have suffered with them covering his entire body. The Bible says he went out and sat in an ash heap and scraped his body with a piece of broken pottery.

His friends came around and decided that Job must have done some terrible things to make God so angry at him. They advised him to repent of his wickedness and maybe God would deliver him.

Job protested his innocense, but nobody listened.

His friends had no comfort for him.

Then Job's wife cracked under the strain. She had seen all of her security destroyed. Her beloved children were all dead. And now, even her husband was stricken. He looked so awful — all swollen and in such terrible misery that she couldn't stand any more. "It's all over," she said to Job. "Why don't you just curse God and die?"

Do you know what Job said? He said, "Good things have come to me, and now bad things. Shall I turn away from God just because things go wrong?"

This didn't mean Job wasn't discouraged. The Bible says he even cursed the day he was born. But he did not sin by turning against God. In spite of all his trouble, Job refused to give up. And God helped him make it through it all.

He wasn't spared the problems.

He wasn't spared the trouble.

He wasn't spared the suffering and pain.

But God brought him through it all. He delivered him from the bad circumstances that came his way. He helped him overcome what men — even loved ones — could do to him. He even delivered him from the evil Job had brought upon himself.

Check up on yourself

God will do the same for you. He loves you as much as He loved Job. He is concerned about everything that touches your life. He sees, He knows, He cares. And when you've reached the bottom...when the night is its blackest, He is there to stretch out His loving hand to you. He speaks the words you need to hear — "Don't give up, My child, you can make it!"

When bad things keep happening to you, make sure you are not contributing to your own trouble. Job was able to examine himself and see that he was not guilty of the terrible sins his friends accused him of. But as he looked within himself, he did discover a dangerous negative force — fear. *"The thing which I greatly feared is come upon me, and that which I was afraid of is come unto me"* (Job 3:25). Positive faith brings success and victory. Negative faith — fear — produces defeat and failure.

So it's good to check up on yourself. How is your faith? Are you believing and fearing?

No matter what happens in your world, keep on trusting God. *"Trust in the Lord with all thine heart; and lean not unto thine own understanding"* (Proverbs 3:5). God is your Supplier — not men, not possessions, not family or friends, not employer or government. Trust God.

Job said, *"Though he slay me, yet will I trust in him"* (Job 13:15).

Remember that God is alive and He is able. The devil may taunt you by asking, "Where is your God now? Why did He let this happen? Why doesn't He help you?"

When that happens, the best thing to do is say, as Job did, *"For I know that my redeemer liveth, and that he shall stand at the latter day upon the earth...whom I shall see for myself, and mine eyes shall behold, and not another"* (Job 19: 25, 27).

Not only is God alive, but He is able to meet your need — to solve your problem. *"The things which are impossible with men are possible with God"* (Luke 18:27).

Know that God is on your side. Job said, *"Now, behold, my witness is in heaven, and my record is on high"* (Job 16:19). He could say with the psalmist David, *"God is our refuge and strength, a very present help in trouble"* (Psalm 46:1).

It hurts when friends forsake you, when loved ones fail. Sometimes it may seem everyone is against you, and you are alone. But God never forsakes you — He is always for you. And *"If God be for us, who can be against us?"* (Romans 8:31).

Tell yourself, God knows and understands! In the middle of his ordeal, Job came to a wonderful realization about God. *"But he knoweth the way that I take: when he hath tried me, I shall come forth as gold"* (Job 23:10).

And God knows all about you, too. He sees everything that is happening, and He understands exactly how you feel. *"For we have not an high priest which cannot be touched with the feeling of our infirmities; but was in all points tempted like as we are, yet without sin. Let us therefore come boldly unto the throne of grace, that we may obtain mercy, and find grace to help in time of need"* (Hebrews 4:15, 16).

You are loved

God loves you, He really does. Do you remember how instinctively one loves a little baby? God loves you just like that. Do you remember how you loved your little boy or your little girl as he or she began to grow up? God loves you just like that. And think of how you love your wife or husband. Well, that is of God. He loves you just like that. He will never leave you. He'll always take care of you — in life or death, in pain, in sickness, in sorrow, in victory, no matter what. And with the power of God's love working for you, what can defeat you? You have to be victorious, whatever your circumstances may be now.

If you can believe that, then simply love God back. That's the secret of praise — loving God...thanking God for what He has promised and what He is doing. Praise opens doors for you, and makes the way plain before

73

you. Praise is the shortest route out of the valley.

So praise God. Give Him thanks.

And pray for others. Jesus taught us to *"pray for them which despitefully use you, and persecute you"* (Matthew 5:44). Hundreds of years before, Job found that praying for others could stop bad things from happening and restore the blessing of God in his life. Job 42:10 tells the story — *"Then, when Job prayed for his friends, the Lord restored his wealth and happiness! In fact, the Lord gave him twice as much as before!"* (Living Bible). Job even got seven more sons and three more daughters. The Bible says God blessed Job more at the end of his life than at the beginning.

Try the praise route! *"For the Lord is great, and greatly to be praised'* (Psalm 96:4).

I have been on the mountaintop. I have been in the valley. I like the mountaintop better. But I am no longer afraid of the valley. When I find myself there, I know I can make it out. I know how to find the shortest route back to the mountaintop — through praise.

Tammy likes to remind herself — and me — that it takes two mountains to make one valley! So you can expect to be "on top" at least twice as often as you're in the valley.

But wherever you are today — keep on praising God. Because you can make it!

Chapter Five

You Can Make It
Through Sickness

Sickness is big business in America today.
There are multiplied thousands of doctors and
medical specialists...almost all of them busy.

There are thousands of clinics, hospitals, and
medical centers...most of them full.

There are drugstores on half the corners of every
business district — drug departments in every super-
market — all doing a land office business selling millions
of dollars worth of pills and potions, drugs and devices.

I don't mean for that to sound critical — it's just a
fact. What it means is that there are more sick people
today than ever before. There are more diseases, more
maladies, and more pain than at any time in history.

In our age of advanced scientific technology, with
all the new wonder drugs and medicines, with improved
sanitation, hygiene, and nutrition, mankind is still not
well. Disease has not been wiped out. Modern medicine
has not destroyed sickness.

And despite years of preaching and teaching by a
great host of outstanding men of God, multitudes of
people are still confused or uncertain about the divine
attitude toward their health. There are literally millions
of books, tapes, tracts, and articles about healing being
distributed each year. Yet suffering people still believe
the devil's deceptions. They write to me every day —
they call PTL's phone counselors at all hours of the day
and night — to ask the same heart-breaking question.
"I'm sick, I'm hurting, I'm desperate," they say. "I
don't think I can take anymore. Is there any hope for

me...would it do any good to pray? IS IT GOD'S WILL TO HEAL?''

I've talked with many of the world's leading evangelists who have appeared on the Jim Bakker program with me and they report that they encounter the same deplorable situation everywhere they go. People somehow are convinced that God gets some glory out of their pain. They believe that some people are healed, but they just aren't sure if God wants them or their loved ones to get well!

If you are to make it through sickness — and you can — you must get some important matters settled in your mind once and for all. You need to know what the Word of God has to say about sickness and healing.

God wants to heal you

Very early in Jesus' public ministry as He traveled throughout Galilee, a leper came to Him. The event is so significant that three of the four Gospel writers include it in their narratives. Why? Because leprosy was the ultimate sickness! It was the most loathsome, feared, and deadly disease that could strike a person in those days. It was the mark of death.

Lepers were cast out of society. They could not touch anybody else and had to cry out a warning if anyone came near — "unclean, unclean."

This particular leper apparently heard passersby talking about a teacher named Jesus. They said that not only did He teach the Scriptures with great power and authority, He also was a healer. Everywhere He went, sick people were brought to Him and He made them well.

"I wish I could meet this Jesus," thought the leper. "Maybe He would have compassion on me."

Then one day Jesus did come to the town where the

leper lived. Crowds thronged about Him as He walked along.

The leper saw Jesus, and suddenly went into action. He forgot about keeping away from other people. He forgot about calling out, "unclean," as the crowd went by. Nothing was important to him at that moment except getting the attention of Jesus.

He burst through the crowd and made his way forward until he found himself face-to-face with the Son of God. Mark's Gospel tells it like this — *"And there came a leper to him, beseeching him, and kneeling down to him, and saying unto him, If thou wilt, thou canst make me clean"* (Mark 1:40).

The leper's words have echoed down through the centuries, repeated again and again by sick and suffering humanity. "Oh Jesus, I'm sick, I'm dying. I know You have the power to help me, to cleanse me, to heal me and make me whole. Will You do it? Is it Your will?"

And Jesus' answer to the leper has also pealed and reverberated to every suffering one who would hear for almost two thousand years now — "I WILL: BE THOU CLEAN."

The Bible says Jesus was moved with compassion and stretched out His hand and touched the leper. And immediately the leprosy departed and the man was cleansed (see Mark 1:40-42). Jesus told the leper, "You can make it! It is My will that you be healed."

And that is His message to you today.

The Bible says that Jesus went about doing good, and healing all that were oppressed of the devil (Acts 10:38). He came to destroy the works of the devil (1 John 3:8). Was it God's will for this to be done?

It must have been, for Jesus declared, *"For I came down from heaven, not to do mine own will, but the will of him that sent me"* (John 6:38). He explained to his disciples, *"The Father that dwelleth in me, he doeth the works. He that hath seen me hath seen the Father"* (John 14:10, 9).

When Jesus Christ came in the flesh to man, teaching about the Kingdom of God, healing the sick, forgiving sin, casting out devils, He was expressing the divine will of God. The Father in heaven was saying, "Hear that! I am speaking to you. When you see Him, you see Me. When you feel His power, you feel My power. He is the brightness of My glory, the express image of My personality. He is My Word to you."

Sickness does not come from God

The Bible teaches that sickness and disease is the work of the devil, of Satan himself. The Old Testament tells how he tried to make himself equal with God and was cast out of heaven. Not being about to strike back at God, the devil and his vast host of demons attack the thing closest to the heart of God — His ultimate creation, mankind. The devil attacks man to try and hurt God.

All disease, all sickness, all pain, and all trouble have their origin in Satan's hatred of God and the human race. Throughout the Bible there are many references to sickness being caused by the devil and his demonic forces. The Scriptures speak of foul spirits, unclean spirits, spirits of infirmity, as well as a dumb devil, blind and dumb devil, and a dumb and deaf spirit. In fact, sickness is always ascribed to Satan...it is the work of the devil.

But Jesus came to earth to destroy Satan's work. He came to be against sickness and disease. He was deeply moved with compassion when He saw people who were sick and afflicted. He loved them and identified with them in their suffering. He touched them and allowed them to touch Him. He placed healing within their reach.

Did you know that, on the average, one of every seven verses in the Gospels is about healing? It's true. The Gospels tell the story of Jesus' life and ministry, and He devoted two-thirds of His time to ministering to the sick.

Wherever you find Jesus in the Bible, He was either on His way to heal someone, He was actually on the scene bringing healing and deliverance to the needy, or He had just set the captive free and was on his way to help someone else.

Just look at these dynamic verses:

"And Jesus went about all the cities...healing every sickness and every disease among the people" (Matthew 9:35).

"And he cast out the spirits with his word, and healed all that were sick" (Matthew 8:16).

"And great multitudes followed him, and he healed them all" (Matthew 12:15).

Everywhere He went He did good. He reached out to the blind, the deaf, the lame...and made them whole. The sick came to Him and He healed their fevers, their hurts, their injuries. By word and by action He said to each sufferer — "You can make it — be healed!"

I know without a shadow of a doubt that Jesus still heals today. Over the years I have seen many tremendous miracles of healing take place through simple faith in God. A few years ago we had a special time of intensive prayer and intercession for the friends and partners of PTL. So many outstanding testimonies came in that I decided to put them in a book. And we did! That book, containing hundreds and hundreds of

79

testimonies, has been read by many thousands of people all across North America.

The Upper Room— a place of miracles

In July 1982, we dedicated a new prayer facility at Heritage USA — the Upper Room. It is a facsimile of the original Upper Room in Jerusalem where Jesus had the last supper with His disciples and where the Holy Spirit fell upon the 120 on the day of Pentecost. The Upper Room we built is a very special place of prayer. The lower level houses our phone counseling center where people can call for prayer 24 hours a day, 365 days a year. And the Upper Room itself is not open for tours — it is reserved for those who wish to pray.

We built some small prayer closets on one side of the Upper Room so individuals would have privacy to seek God. And we keep a pastor on duty all the time. He is always available to pray and anoint with oil. Twice a day, Holy Communion is served.

Almost everyone who goes into that place comments about the special presence of the Lord they feel there. The very air seems charged with the glory and anointing of the Holy Spirit. And from the first day it was open, the Upper Room has been a place of miracles. Hardly a day goes by that we do not receive a report from some person who has been healed of a serious physical malady.

Of course, there is nothing magic about the building itself. It has no healing qualities. But is is a place where faith is stirred and strengthened — and God honors the promises of His Word.

God still heals today. It is His will for the sick to be healed. And He bestows healing in many different ways.

The apostle James said, *"Every good gift and every perfect gift is from above, and cometh down from the Father"* (James 1:17). This means that all healing — which is a good gift — is from God, no matter how it is carried out.

I appreciate the emphasis my friend Oral Roberts has made over the years on the many different ways God heals. He heals through nature and climate. He heals through medical science, through good doctors and medicine. He heals through understanding and love.

But there is a healing power separate from what any doctor can do — a power different from nature or climate or any other form of healing. That healing comes directly through the supernatural power of God in answer to the prayer of faith.

James said, *"Pray one for another, that ye may be healed...the prayer of faith shall save the sick, and the Lord shall raise him up; and if he have committed sins, they shall be forgiven him"* (James 5:16, 15).

That was the apostle's way of saying, "If you pray for one another, you can make it!"

I could go on listing great healing Scriptures from the Word of God. The Bible is a healing book. It teaches that God wants to heal you...that He has promised to heal you. And we know that *"there hath not failed one word of all his good promise"* (1 Kings 8:56). So it really comes down to whether or not you believe the Bible.

Did God say He would heal you?

Do you believe God's Word?

Does God lie or tell the truth?

The great man of God, F.F. Bosworth, once said, "Instead of saying, 'pray for me,' many people should first say, 'Teach me God's Word, so that I can intelligently cooperate with God for my recovery.' "

Receive the healing you need from God. Simply say, *"Heal me, O Lord, and I shall be healed; save me, and I shall be saved"* (Jeremiah 17:14). You can make it through sickness. You can be among that glorious number David wrote about when he said, *"He sent his word, and healed them, and delivered them from their destruction"* (Psalm 107:20).

How to receive your healing

Let me give you some suggestions on how to receive your healing from God:

First, know that God wants to heal you. He wants you to make it through sickness. We've already talked about all the Bible proofs of this truth.

The second thing is that you must want to be healed! Believe it or not, there are some people who really don't want to be healed of their sickness. They get too much satisfaction from the attention they get with it. So they go along, wallowing in self-pity, endlessly reciting their symptoms to anyone who will listen.

To be healed by the power of God, you must want to be healed enough to accept it. Jesus went to a man one day who had been crippled for 38 years. He asked that poor sufferer, *"Wilt thou be made whole?"* (John 5:6). In other words, "Do you really want to be healed?"

When He was satisfied that the man was ready for his miracle, Jesus said, "Rise, take up thy bed, and walk." And immediately the man was made whole.

The third suggestion I have for you is to find the faith that is within you. Don't cop out by saying, "I know God would heal me if I just had more faith." You already have all the faith you need — just use it! The Bible says, *"God hath dealt to every man the measure of faith"* (Romans 12:3). That's why you can make it through sickness. You have *the measure* of faith. It is already within you. Find it — use it...and be healed.

Fourth, accept victory as your answer. When you have prayed in faith, burn every bridge between you and the old affliction. Say with the prophet Isaiah, *"With His stripes I am healed"* (see Isaiah 53:5). Remember, you are healed according to your faith, not according to your feeling. Claim your healing in confidence.

And fifth, remember to give God the praise and thanks for your healing. It is important to give Him the glory, for He alone is able to heal. On one occasion, Jesus healed ten lepers and sent them on their way. Only one came back to express his gratitude. *"Were there not ten cleansed?"* Jesus asked. *"Where are the nine?"* (Luke 17:17).

One last thing — there are no "hard cases" with God. Nothing is impossible with Him. He created your body...certainly He can heal it.

And if you are concerned about the sickness of a loved one, remember that Jesus loves them even more than you do. He wants them to be well. He wants to heal them. He is saying to them even now, "Be healed...you can make it!"

Chapter Six
Making It With Your Finances

Are you facing a financial crisis today?
Millions of people are across our nation. Inflation, recession, and unemployment have left many on the brink of financial disaster.

But there is hope. If you're struggling to make ends meet, God's Word tells you how you can make it financially. The secret of financial success is found in Malachi 3:8-11:

"Will a man rob God? Yet ye have robbed me. But ye say, Wherein have we robbed thee? In tithes and offerings. Ye are cursed with a curse: for ye have robbed me, even this whole nation.

"Bring ye all the tithes into the storehouse, that there may be meat in mine house, and prove me now herewith, saith the Lord of hosts, if I will not open you the windows of heaven, and pour you out a blessing, that there shall not be room enough to receive it.

"And I will rebuke the devourer for you sakes, and he shall not destroy the fruits of your ground; neither shall your vine cast her fruit before the time in the field, saith the Lord of hosts."

Can you imagine God almighty being so upset that he says through His prophet Malachi, "Prove Me. I dare you!" He is upset because His people have robbed Him, and in so doing, robbed themselves of His blessing. They've allowed a curse to come upon themselves.

The people to whom Malachi spoke weren't giving their tithes and offerings to God. *Tithes* means "a tenth." God tells us in His Word that a tithe, or ten percent, of all we own belongs to Him, and we're to give it to Him. But these people refused to give God their tithe, and consequently, the sacred service was interrupted. There wasn't enough money coming in to take care of the priests or the Temple. The people had let their service to God and to the house of the Lord fall by the wayside.

You can't rob God

No doubt these people felt that they had good reasons why they couldn't give. Maybe they had lost their jobs or times were hard or they had too many bills. And so they felt like they couldn't afford to give God their tithes and offerings.

Let me tell you, friend, you can't rob God and get away with it. And when you don't give God your tithes and offerings that is exactly what you're doing — robbing God! And it will bring a curse on you.

You show me someone who robs God and I'll show you trouble, trouble, trouble. I'll show you some mean, despondent, suicidal people. I'll show you people who are having nothing but problems. They're in and out of every hospital. Their kids are in trouble. Their lives are unhappy. They may not be paying their tithes to God, but they're paying them to someone.

Several months ago one of my accountants decided he was going to borrow from PTL's tithe fund, which is used for missions projects, to pay some ministry bills. This is strictly against my rules and principles, but he felt we had to have the money. A few months later I was looking at the records and I said, "How come you borrowed from the tithe fund?"

He said, "I didn't have enough money to pay the bills, so I had to."

I said, "Never touch God's money. Even if we can't pay all our bills, don't ever take money from the tithe fund."

I started checking and you know what I discovered? During that period of time we had lost the exact amount of money *to the dollar* that we had borrowed from God's money. You see, we still paid that tithe money, but we paid it to someone else.

When you rob God, it's going to come out of your hide! That's rough, isn't it? But it's the truth. Withholding from the Lord will place you under a curse of misfortune. You're going to have more trouble, more bills, more emergencies than you know what to do with. That money you thought you would save by not paying your tithes will have to go to pay these extra expenses. You will never come out ahead that way.

You can have a flood of blessing

But when you start giving God your tithes, He has promised to bless you abundantly. He said, *"Prove me now herewith...if I will not open you the windows of heaven, and pour you out a blessing, that there shall not be room enough to receive it"* (Malachi 3:10).

"Pour you out" means "empty out upon." God is saying, "I'm going to give you the whole blessing, the whole bucketful. I will pour it out upon you. I will open the windows of heaven and pour you out a blessing so big you won't know what to do with it all."

God used this same term about the windows of heaven over in Genesis 7:11, 12: *"In the six hundredth year of Noah's life, in the second month, the seventeenth day of the month, the same day were all the fountains of the great deep broken up, and the windows of heaven*

86

were opened. And the rain was upon the earth forty days and forty nights.''

Did they have a nice little Spring rain in Noah's day? Did they have "showers of blessing?" The old gospel song says, "Showers of blessing we need, Mercy drops 'round us are falling..." Well, let me tell you, they didn't have mercy drops of Spring showers in Noah's day. They had an inundating flood that covered everything. The windows of heaven were opened and God poured out a flood upon the earth that covered all.

In Malachi 3:10, God is saying, "I've got another kind of flood I want to give you. If you'll straighten up and do what I told you, I'll open the windows of heaven and pour you out a blessing that you won't have room enough to contain. Not a trickle, not a Spring rain, not mercy drops — but a flood of blessings in your life.''

If you've been robbing God, He is telling you, "I want to give you a flood. I want to give you something that's going to change your life. You're already cursed with a curse. You can't seem to get ahead. But if you'll put me first and obey Me...if you'll bring your tithes and offerings into My storehouse, I'm going to empty out a blessing upon you that will be more than enough to meet your needs.''

Give to God first

You say, "I'm ready for the flood! I'm ready for God to pour me out a blessing."

Have you done what He told you to do? You have a part in this, too. God made a commitment that He would bless you, but first you've got to do something — you've got to give to God. And then He'll give back to you.

It's like a farmer planting a field. He can go out to that field and say, "Okay, field. I'm ready. Give me some grain." But if he hasn't planted any seed, he's not going to get any grain. First he has to plant his seed, and then he can expect a harvest.

That's what the scripture is all about. Give — and then you will receive. First you give your best — your tithes and offerings — to God. You plant your financial seeds of faith. And then God gives you an abundant harvest of blessings.

Jesus said in Luke 6:38, *"Give, and it shall be given unto you; good measure, pressed down, and shaken together, and running over."* Do you see who is supposed to act first here? You are. You give, and God gives back to you.

Just a decade ago the PTL ministry had one TV station and we were in a rented furniture store. Every year since has been a bigger financial year than the one before. Why? Because each year we gave more than we had ever given before. And we got back more than we ever had in our history.

I'm telling you, it works! The month I decided I was going to give God more than I'd ever given Him before in my life was the month we received the biggest income in the history of this ministry. We got a literal flood of blessing.

And it will work for you, too. Not only is God going to bless you, but Malachi 3:11 says He will rebuke the devourer for your sake so he will not destroy the fruit of your ground. This means the devil can't destroy your blessing. He'll try, but the Lord is going to give you a blessing the devil can't destroy.

Who gets your tithe?

Now, a lot of people are confused about who they're supposed to give their tithes and offerings to. Let me tell you — *give them to God*. They're His. If you want to know how much money to give to each church or ministry, ask God about it. He'll tell you what He wants you to do with His money.

Just because something sounds wonderful doesn't necessarily mean that's what God wants for you. It might seem wonderful for you to help build a new sanctuary for your local church, but maybe that isn't what God wants right now. It would be wonderful for you to help build a home for troubled children in your community, but maybe it's not God's will for you to do that. Maybe He has some other jobs for you to do.

You need to find out what God wants you to do and do it. Support those ministries that bless you and help you. If you attend a local church — and I hope you do — support it with your tithes. If you feel PTL ministers to you and you believe in what we're doing, then support us and help us stay on the air.

Whatever you give to God, He will give back to you many times over. That's the secret of financial success — you can't outgive God. The more you give to Him, the more He gives back to you.

Are you going through a financial struggle in your life? Start giving to God. Don't give Him what's left after the bills have been paid; give Him your best first. And He promises He'll help you make it, no matter what the economy is doing, or your job is doing, or your bills are doing. He'll bless you abundantly so that you can make it financially.

How to use what God gives you

There's no question about it — giving to God will generate a flow of blessing into your life. But if you want to make it with your finances, it's important to manage and use your income wisely. No matter how much you have coming in, you'll still go broke if you keep spending more than that.

An old farmer once summed up the basics of poor economics by saying, "If your outgo is more than your income, your upkeep will be your downfall!" And that's exactly true. Most of the people who go bankrupt don't go under because they have too little income — they just don't manage it will. They overextend themselves by spending too much too fast...by committing themselves to more "easy payments" than they can cover.

Failure to use money wisely causes more heartache and trouble than you can imagine. Some time ago *The Ladies' Home Journal* reported that more than seventy percent of our modern worries are about money. A national association of family counselors has estimated that ninety-percent of divorces are finance-related.

Planning how to use your money may be more important than the money itself. In any endeavor, having a plan is essential to success. No building is ever begun without a blueprint. No project can hope to be successful without a plan of action.

Robert Schuller, speaker on the *Hour of Power* and the builder of the famed Crystal Cathedral in Southern California, says — *"Failing to plan is planning to fail!"*

You can make it with your finances...but you need a plan. That plan is called a budget. You may not like the sound of that word, but a good budget can be one of the best friends you'll ever have. Family financial planners say that any household without a budget is wasting from 10 to 30 percent of its income — sometimes even more.

There came a time when the Lord really dealt with me about setting up a definite, detailed budget for PTL. We've always tried hard to be good stewards of the funds God has entrusted to our management. I can't stand waste, and I've always been sensitive about making every dollar of God's money go as far as possible.

But the growth of our ministry has been so rapid and the scope of our outreaches has spread so quickly that we've often found ourselves facing a financial crisis before we knew it. When you're building new facilities, obtaining the equipment a television ministry must have, expanding station coverage, developing a major Christian satellite — cable network, and supporting missions projects around the world, even a small change in projected income or the national economy can be devastating.

I found myself spending much of my time trying to bail PTL out of financial crisis. Each emergency seemed worse than the one before. I was frustrated because our financial problems were not the result of waste or bad use of funds.   But again and again I had to go to my friends and Partners for special help — on TV and in the mail. Thank God, they always came through.

But I felt it was not good to always be in financial trouble. And as I prayed for God's help and guidance, He led me to set up a new budgeting system for the ministry. I went over the entire ministry, department by department. Anything that could be changed to save money or be more efficient was done. Anywhere I could find duplication of effort or unnecessary activities — I cut!

Working with the people in charge of each department, I determined how much money was absolutely necessary to keep that part of the ministry operating. That amount became the budget for that department. If the amount still seemed too large, in some cases we cut back on the activities of that department to fit what we felt we could afford. We went through the whole ministry that way, and each manager was charged not to spend one dollar more than was allocated to his department's budget. No expense above that — no matter how worthy — would be approved.

In the past when good and worthwhile opportunities came along, the temptation was to take them on without knowing how they would be funded. Now no project can be begun without our being sure there are funds in some part of the budget to cover it!

That doesn't mean PTL will not and does not take on new ventures by faith! If God says to do it, we go ahead. But at least we do it knowing that we need a financial miracle to get the job done. And we can pray and plan accordingly.

You need a budget too. It may be a simple one, but it is important for you to have a definite plan for the money God places in your hands.

There are many fine Christian books available on Christian money management. Two good ones are George Bowman's *How To Succeed With Your Money* and Malcolm McGregor's *Your Money Matters*. Both authors recommend a budget system called the 10-70-20 plan. It's a sound and simple system you should consider.

Essentially, the 10-70-20 plan is this: after paying your tithes and standard taxes, save ten percent of the balance, live on seventy percent, and use twenty percent to pay debts.

You may have to make some radical changes in your lifestyle to live by your budget. But it will be worth it. It will take away the stress and strain of constantly being in financial straits and will help you become financially free.

Put God first and give Him your best. Then make a good budget and manage the rest. That may not be good poetry, but it is good advice. It can help you make it with your finances!

Remember, God's will for your financial success is

unmistakably clear. His Word declares, *"Beloved, I wish above all things that thou mayest prosper and be in health, even as thy soul prospereth"* (3 John 2).

Chapter Seven
You Can Make It With Your Family

America is under seige today!

Our beloved nation is facing an attack so vicious and so deadly that some expert observers are seriously questioning if she can survive.

The enemy is not Russia with its military might and growing stockpile of nuclear weapons.

The deadly threat does not come from a faltering national economy, lessened productivity, or staggering unemployment.

The destructive danger is the disintegration of the American family!

More than a million marriages in the United States will fall apart this year. Divorce destroys more than one third of all marriages, striking even Christian homes.

Living together without getting married is no longer considered shameful. Such couples even have children with no fear of social stigma.

Homosexuals flaunt their perversion and make mockery of the sacrament of marriage by exchanging public wedding vows — men marrying men and women wedding women.

And the stress and tension of our fast-paced way of life puts pressure on almost all the "normal" homes. We are a nation on the go, with every day crammed full of activities that keep dad, mom, and the kids scattered in different directions from morning until past bedtime!

For a variety of reasons, more and more women go out into the business world every day to help earn the family income. Some do it out of apparent necessity —

others want to afford more and better "things" —
others to escape what they consider the confinement of
staying at home.

This means the children go to a babysitter or
nursery, or come home from school to an empty house.
As they grow older, youngsters get involved in school
activities, music lessons, sports and clubs. There's
nothing wrong with any of these things, except they
take the children away from home and parents more
and more.

Husbands and fathers keep busy too. If they're not
workaholics, staying late at the office or bringing home
a bulging briefcase every night, there are always things
to do outside, meetings to attend, or sports programs to
watch on television.

The end result is there is very little family life.
There is just a group of individuals scurrying about, too
busy to spend time together, too tired to talk. And when
the weariness, loneliness, and anxiety have built up
enough, the slightest crisis can destroy a marriage and
shatter a home. Afterward, the poor victims may not
even know for sure what happened.

Yes, America's families are in danger. More and
more homes are being destroyed by what philosophers
call "the acids of modernity."

But it doesn't have to be that way. Your home
doesn't have to be a victim. Your marriage can survive.
Your children can grow up strong and well, physically,
emotionally, and spiritually.

PTL's new ministry to families

For the last several years I have been interested in
Christian families. I've had a burden to help them with
the needs and problems they face in surviving. I've
looked into the faces of many of the people who have

come to Heritage USA and seen the hurt and bewilderment they felt.

So often I sensed that these people were hurting and in need, wounded in their relationships with each other. They came — many in desperation, as a last resort — because they'd heard that PTL cares about families. They came hoping to find answers and relief for the hurts in their lives.

The PTL ministerial staff tried to help them. We did all we could. We listened, we prayed, we shared God's Word...we just loved them as best we could. And many were helped.

But I could see that others needed more help than we were equipped to give them. They needed practical help in applying God's principles to their lives, including viable suggestions and demonstrations of how God's way really works.

So we launched a major new PTL ministry. Under the guidance of the Holy Spirit, we established a Total Learning Center, complete with its own facility and highly qualified staff. It was opened in January, 1983.

I felt there should be a place where troubled Christian families could go for help. The sole purpose of our center is to help the family — to increase its stability, its support, its growth, and its protection in a world bent on tearing it apart.

The center provides guidance and instruction for the family as a whole and for individual members, married, single, adolescent, and elderly. Teaching seminars by top Christian leaders and teachers are being offered on a variety of topics.

People need to learn how to become better husbands and wives, how to make their marriages work, and how to train their children. Proverbs 22:6 says to *"train up a child in the way he should go,"* but how do you do that? We are showing people how.

In addition to teaching seminars, PTL's Total Learning Center also offers monthly two or three day workshops which are intensive training sessions. Workshops provide basic scriptural training combined with role playing, group exercises, and individual participation.

These sessions are directed by Dr. Fred Gross of California's Palmdale General Hospital, who founded the Christian Therapy Program there, and our resident director, Vi Azvedo, who formerly was a counselor at Palmdale General. These two outstanding specialists are assisted by an experienced teaching team.

Two workshops that are having dramatic results are the Personal Growth Workshop, which focuses on understanding your emotions and learning how to change your behavior, and the Marriage Enrichment Workshop, which emphasizes the development of relationship skills.

The family Total Learning Center is available to anyone who needs special help. I want you to know that I care about you and your family, and this new PTL ministry is ready to help you should the need arise.

You are not alone. Someone does care. You CAN make it with your family.

The key of communication

Perhaps the single most important thing to do to help your family is to keep the lines of communication open. Husbands and wives must talk to each other. Parents and children must be able to say what's on their mind. There is something about sharing one's feelings with someone you love that bonds you closer together and strengthens your relationship. It's important to share excitement, joy, pride, hopes, and goals, as well as concerns, needs, problems, and disappointments.

And it's also important to teach your family to communicate with God — to share everything with Him. Dr. Richard Dobbins, one of America's outstanding Christian psychologists, emphasizes the importance of prayer to families. In a study of 237 Christian married adults, ranging in age from 25 to 65, the number one problem detected was in communication. And over fifty percent of those who identified a lack of communication as their primary problem said they and their marriage partner never prayed together, or did so only occasionally.

Dr. Dobbins says, "The absence of prayer among couples is the greatest spiritual weakness they face today.

"As far as the family as a whole is concerned," he said, "it is vitally important that couples cultivate the ability to express themselves to God, to each other, and to their children. When children observe parents praying, it makes God and their parents more approachable to them."

There is a great deal of truth to the old proverb that says, "The family that prays together, stays together."

Five suggestions to help you make it with your family

Let me offer some practical, common sense suggestions that can help you make it in your marriage and your family.

First, *be sure to make time to be together as a family.* Don't ever get too busy for each other. I've always made it a rule in my office that Tammy or the children can call me whenever they need to. I can be interrupted in *any* meeting to talk to them. The demands on my time and

Tammy's are enormous. We both work very hard during the week but we always try to save weekends for special times with all four of us. We all talk and hug and kiss a lot — we enjoy each other.

Second, *try and find time to pray with your mate every day.* The time to start this practice is before you get married. But if you didn't and you still don't have a daily prayer time together — begin today.

As you talk to God with each other, and about each other, divine love covers the spots where your own love may be stretched a bit thin. And you'll find it's pretty easy to get over feeling quarrelsome toward your marriage partner when you're praying for him or her.

Daily prayer will have the same good results with your children, too. Lots of potential problems just never happen when you pray about them first.

Third, *your family should worship together.* Worship is the joyous acknowledgment of the involvement of God in our lives. It is recognizing His greatness, and accepting anew His call to service. Church should be a regular part of your family's life.

Husbands and wives should worship God together. Parents should take — not send — their children to church. That may not be startling new information and advice. But it is the best guidance I can possibly give you to help you and your family make it!

My fourth suggestion is, *Love your husband or wife and your children as Christ loves.* And how is that?

"Love is very patient and kind, never jealous or envious, never boastful or proud, never haughty or selfish or rude. Love does not demand its own way. It is not irritable or touchy. It does not hold grudges and will hardly even notice when others do it wrong. It is never glad about injustice, but rejoices whenever truth wins out. If you love someone you will be loyal to him no matter what

the cost. You will always believe in him, always expect the best of him, and always stand your ground in defending him" (1 Corinthians 13:4-7, The Living Bible).

Go back over that list again. Is that a good description of the way you love? Are there some things you need to change in your loving relationship to your family? You can be sure that as you begin to love in this way, the other members of your family will respond and will begin to love you in the same way.

Fifth, *don't panic when problems come.* Working together, you can solve them. Life with no challenges would get pretty dull.

The most important thing is to keep communicating. That means one person must be listening at all times. And don't forget that the goal is to solve the problem, not just win an argument or get your own way.

The more problems you solve together, the stronger you become and the more confidence you have in each other.

"Train up a child..."

When I got started in the ministry, I made a startling discovery. As I preached and taught, I got more out of my sermons and lessons than anyone else. At first I thought this was the result of my own inexperience, but it continues to happen to me. And many other ministers have told me the same thing happens to them. When they teach, they learn the most.

Well, this happens to parents too. In fact, I'm convinced that one of the reasons God says to train up a child in the way he should go is that He knows the parents will stumble onto the right road in the bargain.

Tammy and I don't really have any special secrets or gems of knowledge to impart about raising children.

100

We're still learning! We just try to love our children as much as we can, and we teach them to love the Lord.

Sometimes we make mistakes, and we admit to Jamie and Tammy Sue when we are wrong. But as parents, we stick together on decisions, and try not to allow the kids to pit us against one another. Jesus said, *"And if a house be divided against itself, that house cannot stand"* (Mark 3:25).

Just as communication is vital to a happy marriage, so it is important to your relationship with your children. I've never understood why a parent would clam up and give a son or daughter the "silent treatment" when he was upset. Withholding approval from a child because he isn't satisfying you is like refusing to shine a light into a room because it's too dark. That kind of behavior short-circuits the flow of love into a child's life and deprives him of the opportunity to be inspired and restored to the fold of love and acceptance once more.

One more suggestion. When you pray for your child, don't be negative. Don't complain to God about all the bad things and disappointments your youngster causes. Instead, pray affirmations of the good things you expect. You'll be amazed at how much better results you get from that kind of praying.

Remember, also, to think loving thoughts about your children. Try writing love notes to them. Whether or not you ever deliver them, the act of writing those notes will change your whole mental attitude. And because love is spiritual in nature, it will travel to your children wherever they are, and bless them.

You can get along with your children better. You can influence their lives and win them for the Lord. And you can change a troubled marriage for the better, or improve an already good one. You can make it with your family. That's what God wants for you.

I especially like what Pat Boone said about the family in his book, *Together, 25 Years With The Boone Family*. He wrote: "God seems to be especially interested in this family thing. When you get right down to it, the whole thing was His idea, and He seems to know how it works best. You can try some other way if you want to, but you'll risk losing it all and settle for second best, if you survive.

"I don't know how a family can make it today in this turbulent and treacherous world without the Lord. I hope you won't feel it's presumptuous of me to recommend to you the Manufacturer's Handbook, the Bible. It's also the marriage manual, the family encyclopedia, the ultimate source on raising kids, the essential guide for life, happiness, and real fulfillment."

Good advice. I recommend it to you today. And as you look into the pages of God's Word, you'll find little reminders everywhere that...

You can make it with your family!

Chapter Eight
Making It Out Of Depression

Do you ever get depressed?

Most of us do at one time or another in our life. In fact, emotional depression is probably the most common symptom of unhappiness in our country today.

Experts predict that one out of eight Americans will be so seriously affected by depression that they can no longer help themselves and will require professional treatment. In any one year, between four and eight million American citizens are depressed to the extent that they cannot function effectively at their jobs.

Depression affects rich and poor, men and women, young and old, **unsaved and Christian.** That's right — depression strikes believers. And despite what you may have heard or been taught, depression is not a sin or a punishment for transgression!

Several years ago *Newsweek* magazine devoted its cover and lead article to the subject, titling its study, "Coping With Depression." *Newsweek* stated, "There is no doubt that depression, long the leading mental illness in the U.S., is now virtually epidemic — and suicide is its all too frequent outcome."

You may be sure the situation has not gotten any better since that was written. Depression is still a major problem, not only in America, but around the world. And, as a matter of fact, depression can be a killer — and is! Studies show that suicide ranks as the fifth largest killer of Americans in the fifteen to fifty-five age group. And over eighty percent of all suicide victims are deeply depressed.

What is depression?

Webster defines depression as being pressed down, gloomy, defected, sad, to have low spirits. He also says, "Psychological depression is an emotional condition characterized by discouragement and the feeling of inadequacy."

What causes it?

There may be almost as many different causes as there are people. Some of the more common ones include fatigue, improper diet, self-pity, negative thinking, illness, repressed anger, and lack of self-esteem.

What cures it?

Real depression, as opposed to the temporary "blues" we all wrestle with from time to time, usually requires some kind of therapy — psychotherapy, drug therapy, electrotherapy, or spiritual therapy. Whistling in the dark won't work. Ignoring our feelings and hoping they'll go away is not enough. Trying to pull ourselves up by our bootstraps is impossible.

But as Christians, you and I have something special going for us. We have the unlimited resources of heaven at our disposal and the healing love of our Lord and Saviour to draw upon. And as we look into the Scriptures, we discover that God has made it possible for us to deal realistically with our depression. At the lowest ebb of our existence, in the darkest hour of our nightmarish ordeal, we can hear the still, small voice of God speaking to us —

"You can make it...be of good cheer!"

Depression strikes Elijah

Perhaps the greatest example of depression in the Bible is the story of Elijah. He had been God's spokesman for over three years, faithfully calling the nation back to God. In a dramatic battle with the four hundred and fifty prophets of Baal on Mt. Carmel, Elijah proved he was God's servant. God also affirmed Elijah by answering his prayer to send rain to break a long drought. But as he ran before Ahab's chariot back to Jezreel, the wicked Jezebel sent a message — "By this time tomorrow you'll be dead — I guarantee it!"

Tired, emotionally spent, Elijah heard the threat... and panicked. He forgot the tremendous power God had just demonstrated. He got scared and ran.

The next time we see Elijah he has gone a full day's journey out into the wilderness. He is totally dejected, sitting under a juniper bush. Elijah cries, *It is enough; now, O Lord, take away my life; for I am not better than my fathers"* (1 Kings 19:4).

Someone has pointed out that Elijah's depression was not very reasonable. Even his prayer of utter despair, asking to die, seemed to lack complete sincerity. If Elijah had really wanted to die all he had to do was hang around the palace and Jezebel would have been glad to help him! Nevertheless, his pain and suffering were no less real.

I think there are some important lessons we can learn from Elijah's situation. There are at least four things we can discover about making it out of depression.

First, *when you are depressed, get away for a rest.* This is what Elijah did. After doing a mighty work for God and literally running many miles, he was physically exhausted. He had been so busy caring for the spiritual needs of the nation that he neglected his own. Exhausted, he fell asleep under the juniper bush and had to be awakened twice by an angel to eat. After a good rest and food, he got up and had enough strength to travel forty days and nights to Mount Horeb.

105

Things haven't changed much since Elijah's day. Many still grow weary from well-doing. What begins as a fun or joyful ministry often becomes a wearying grind. When this happens it does us good to get away for an unhindered period of rest. Often just one good night's sleep away from a problem will do wonders for our mental attitude.

What I learned about depression

I learned about the consequences of not getting enough rest the hard way. In May 1969, after four years of long hours and constant pressures at CBN where I was working, I went home one night and collapsed. My nerves couldn't take any more. I felt like I was coming apart. I couldn't talk to anybody. I only wanted to be away from people.

I was dizzy. I couldn't sleep. I couldn't eat. The slightest little problem seemed completely impossible to me. I sensed that I was right on the edge — that my grip on self-control might snap at any minute.

The doctor I consulted tried various medications. They didn't help — if anything, they made me feel worse. I was put on a special cream and milk diet, and for more than a month I couldn't work. I stayed home while Tammy and others did the two daily television shows I had been hosting.

I remember so well that during that month I thought I'd never be better — that there was no way out for me. I cried out to God for help, but my progress was so slow. I learned about depression.

During those long days, I tried to read the Word of God when my nerves would permit me to concentrate. Leafing through my Bible one day, I came across some notes I'd made about a prophecy that had been given over Tammy and me at the very beginning of our ministry. One sentence leaped out at me — "The Lord wants you to get plenty of rest, if you don't, the devil will use it against you."

God had warned me eight years before, but I had failed to heed it. I had pushed on. For years I had not gotten enough rest, had not eaten properly. And for breaking God's fixed laws, I eventually had a breakdown.

Since then I've tried to use more wisdom. I still work hard. There are times when the load gets heavy and the pressure builds up. But when I feel the numbness of fatigue creeping over my body, I stop and rest. Sometimes Tammy and I get out of town for a day or two to let God restore our strength and renew our minds.

And when you find yourself struggling often with bone-tiredness and its accompanying discouragement, take time out to rest. It is one of the ways you can make it out of depression.

The second thing to do to combat depression is to *get your frustrations off your chest.* After Elijah had slept, eaten, and traveled forty more days to the cave in Horeb, the Lord came to him there. He said, "What are you doing here, Elijah?" In effect, God was saying, "Elijah, tell me what's bothering you."

And Elijah did. He took this opportunity to pour out his frustrations. He said, *"Lord, those people didn't appreciate a thing I did. Even when the drought was broken they were against me. In fact, they're looking for me right now to kill me. Furthermore, I'm the only servant you've got left and it looks like I'm wasting my time. There's no use living anymore. I may as well die and get it over with"* (see 1 Kings 19:9, 19).

In one exasperated moment, Elijah poured out the venom that was poisoning his soul. And without realizing it, he set a workable pattern for you and me to follow — we must get our frustrations out in the open and tell God what's eating us!

God is interested in the things that bother us. He understands our problem and, rather than condemn us, wants to help us overcome our infirmities. He speaks no rebuke, but says, "That's all right — you can make it!"

Most of the time when we get hold of our problem and put it into words, we discover that it is not nearly as big as we thought it was. And that discovery helps us begin moving out of our depression.

The third lesson we can learn from Elijah — *get a fresh awareness of the personal presence of God. In his isolated despair, Elijah began to doubt the power and personal presence of the Lord. He felt forsaken and alone.*

As he stood at the mouth of the cave of Horeb, a great wind came up, so strong it actually split rocks. But the Lord was not in the wind.

Then came an earthquake — but the Lord was not in the earthquake.

After that, a raging fire swept into view — but the Lord was not in the fire.

The Bible says that when these awesome manifestations ended, there was "a still small voice" (1 Kings 19:12). After everything had quieted down, Elijah became aware of God's presence...he could hear His voice again. In a moment the prophet received a fresh awareness of the personal presence and power of God.

When depressed we, too, need a fresh awareness of the presence and power of God in our lives. When we are rejected by friends, it's easy to fall into depths of depression and insulate ourselves from God in a blanket of self-pity. We want God to demonstrate His mighty power so we can sense His presence. Instead, we need to seek God's presence in solitude and quietness because it is here the Lord will meet us with a fresh awareness of His presence.

The fourth thing we can do to defeat depression is to *get back to work*. After resting, after venting his frustrations, after receiving a new awareness of God's presence, Elijah was still sitting around, moping and complaining. God came to him again and told him two important things. The first was to get up and get back to work. The Lord said, *"You have been commissioned to be a prophet, so get going. I need you to anoint two kings and a prophet. It's time for you to get your mind off yourself and start doing my work again"* (see 1 Kings 19:15, 16).

Then God said, *"And by the way, you are not alone in the work of God. There are still seven thousand who remain faithful to Me"* (see verse 18).

When Elijah learned he was not alone in serving God and the others were actively working with him, he overcame his depression and went back on the road to do the job God called him to.

Like Elijah, once we have rested and had a fresh awareness of the presence of God, we must get up off our self-pity and get back to work. Depression is not the end of the world. You can make it out of depression.

There are other examples in the Bible of men of God who struggled with depression. Moses grew depressed by the burden of serving the multitude he had led out of Egypt's bondage. He, too, prayed that God would "do him a favor" and kill him. Instead, God gave Moses some help by dividing the labor among the elders of Israel. Moses' depression soon passed.

David knew what it was to reach the awful depths of depression. Several of the Psalms express the deep mental anguish he felt. But he learned to encourage himself in the Lord and allow God to restore his confidence and faith.

Jesus himself experienced the torture of depression when He went to Gethsemane. *"And taking with Him Peter and the two sons of Zebedee, He began to show grief and distress of mind and was deeply depressed. Then He said to them, My soul is very sad and deeply grieved, so that I am almost dying of sorrow..."* (Matthew 26:37, 38, Amplified Bible).

So don't ever feel that you are the only person who has ever been depressed. And no matter how low your spirits may be, you are not defeated. God will bring you through. You can make it out of depression.

Let the Word of God speak to your heart —

"We are troubled on every side, yet not distressed; we are perplexed, but not in despair; Persecuted, but not forsaken; cast down, but not destroyed" (2 Corinthians 4:8, 9).

"For God hath not given us the spirit of fear; but of power, and of love, and of a sound mind" (2 Timothy 1:7).

"Do not fret or have any anxiety about anything, but in every circumstance and in everything by prayer and petition (definite requests) with thanksgiving continue to make your wants known to God" (Philippians 4:6, Amplified Bible).

"And be constantly renewed in the spirit of your mind — having a fresh mental and spiritual attitude" (Ephesians 4:23, Amplified Bible).

God did not design you to be crippled by depression. He will help you. He will deliver you. You can make it out of depression.

Chapter Nine
Unlimited Power To Help You Make It

The Christian life is a conflict, a fight, a battle. The Bible even speaks of it as warfare. But it is not a flesh-and-blood war. The Word of God says, *"For we wrestle not against flesh and blood, but against principalities, against powers..."* (Ephesians 6:12).

The foe we face is powerful, there's no question about that. Satan has power. The devil is called the *"prince of the power of the air"* (Ephesians 2:2). And he is relentless in his attack on God's children.

Tragically, too often he is able to bind and defeat many Christians, not because he is so strong but because they are not aware of the spiritual power available to them. They are defeated because they think they are weak and powerless.

As a believer, you can defeat the devil. He has no authority over you. You have the right to be victorious over every obstacle, every adversity, and every enemy that opposes you. God has provided *unlimited power* to help you make it. That power is the living, indwelling presence of the Holy Spirit.

The Bible says, *"power belongeth unto God"* (Psalm 62:11). During His earthly ministry, Jesus declared, *"All power is given unto me in heaven and in earth"* (Matthew 28:18). Before He went back to heaven, Jesus told His followers, *"And, behold, I send the promise of my Father upon you: but tarry ye in the city of Jerusalem, until ye be endued with power from on high"* (Luke 24:49).

The Lord also said to His disciples, *"But ye shall receive power, after that the Holy Ghost is come upon you"* (Acts 1:8). Bible scholars tell me that the Greek word for power used in this Scripture is "dunamis." It is derived from a word which signifies ability — the power to accomplish anything. It means inherent ability — "can do" power!

And that is what God had given to you and me. That is why he is saying to true believers today, "You can make it because I have given you unlimited power."

Jesus was anointed to minister. He did mighty miracles through the power of the Holy Spirit. Luke wrote, *"God anointed Jesus of Nazareth with the Holy Ghost and with power: who went about doing good, and healing all that were oppressed of the devil"* (Acts 10:38).

If Jesus relied upon the power of the Holy Ghost for his miraculous ministry, how much more you and I should be empowered by that same source to perform the tasks and to meet the challenges of our time.

My good friend, C.M. Ward, the most popular guest preacher at PTL, is a renowned authority on the Holy Spirit. In his book, *The Holy Spirit Is For You,* he refers to the time when Jesus told His disciples that it was better for them that He go away. *"For if I go not away, the Comforter will not come unto you; but if I depart, I will send him unto you"* (John 16:7). C.M. Ward declared: "Jesus said it was more expedient for His people to have this infilling than that He should remain with them. *That is how important the baptism of the Holy Ghost is to the believer*. It is promised to all believers to the end of time."

You need the power in your life that comes from being baptized in the Holy Spirit. It will produce results. It will make you a winner. It will help you make it in every part of your life.

This is the most exciting time to be alive since the dawn of creation. I firmly believe we are living in the age of the Holy Spirit, the hour of the great outpouring spoken of by the prophets and promised by God the Father. I can sense the move of the Holy Spirit coming to this generation like never before.

I believe in Pentecost

In recent years this stirring of spiritual power has been called the Charismatic Movement. It has been a wonderful era — glorious, marvelous. I have endorsed it, encouraged it, supported it. I love to see people hungry for more of God, and I want everybody to receive the Holy Ghost. We built the Upper Room at Heritage USA as a symbol of Pentecost!

I was a Charismatic before the term was invented — when people who received the infilling of the Holy Spirit were Pentecostals. When I was a child it wasn't popular or even socially acceptable to be Pentecostal. Most of these "fanatics and holy rollers" conducted their services in brush arbors, rag tents, cow sheds, store buildings and little tabernacles — all on the wrong side of town.

I am third generation Assemblies of God, one of the first Pentecostal church movements in the United States. My grandfather founded the Assemblies of God church in Muskegon, Michigan. I grew up hearing dynamic preaching about the power of God in action. I heard that God healed the sick, provided every need, and performed miracles — and I saw those things actually happen.

Despite ridicule, misunderstanding, opposition, and sometimes persecution, the first American Pentecostals kept proclaiming the full gospel — that the baptism in the Holy Spirit was for all believers and should be a normal part of every Christian's experience.

Then it started happening! Presbyterians, Episcopalians, Lutherans, Methodists, Baptists, Catholics — people from all the so-called mainline churches began to receive the Holy Spirit and speak in tongues. And wouldn't you know it, some of the Pentecostals got jealous and almost missed out on the Charismatic revival when it began.

But the revival continues. The move is on! People all around the world are hungry for the Holy Spirit. They are coming to the Pentecostals and saying, "What are you doing? What have you got? How does it work? How can I receive? I'm tired, I'm hungry, I want more of God."

I believe what they want and what the Church of Jesus Christ needs more than anything else is the experience of Pentecost, with tongues of fire from heaven. I'm not ashamed of Pentecost. I'm not ashamed of the Holy Ghost and the power for living He gives.

I am fed up with the things of this world. I'm tired of trying to "fit in" with men's ideas and programs, with the "isms" and gimmicks and all the other stuff. What I want more than anything else is a new Pentecost in my heart and soul, in my ministry, in this world. My heart cries out, "Lord, send the old time power, the Pentecostal power!"

My ministry was born in the fire of Pentecost. It has grown under the anointing and with the direction of the Holy Spirit. The closest I've ever been to failure was when I began to let that fire die down and go out. The devil is not afraid of ashes, and for a couple of years he tried to tromp on me — he tried to take control in different areas and keep me and the PTL ministry from making it.

114

But then God spoke to my heart and showed me it was time to use the power of the Holy Spirit in my life and take authority in the name of Jesus. It was as if He spoke to me and said, "Jim, you can make it...with the unlimited power of the Holy Spirit."

And you can make it too. The Holy Spirit is the power source you need. He is your Comforter, your Helper, your Advocate, your Teacher, your Guide, and your Friend. There is no substitue for the anointing of the Holy Ghost. It is the only thing that will cause you to survive.

The purpose of Pentecost

Some Christians have mistaken ideas about the purpose of Pentecost. There are those who think the primary purpose of the Baptism is to speak with other tongues. I believe in speaking in tongues. I accept it as the initial witness or evidence that the Spirit has come to an individual. And I practice speaking in tongues often as a personal prayer language. But speaking in tongues is not the height of the Holy Ghost experience, it is merely the starting point.

Nor is tongues speaking just a way to experience an ecstatic, emotional high. It is not for sensation. The objective of the Christian is not just to get a blessing, but to be a blessing to others.

The true objective of Pentecost is to empower believers to be victorious in their own lives so they can take Christ to the world. When the Spirit came, the disciples went. They went everywhere and preached Christ. The secret of their success was that "the Spirit gave them utterance." When the Spirit came, He focused attention on Christ. Anyone who possesses the Holy Spirit baptism will do likewise.

This was the program of the early Church — *"And*

daily in the temple, and in every house, they ceased not to teach and preach Jesus Christ" (Acts 5:42). Wherever they went, they continued the work and ministry of Jesus, loving people and destroying the work of the devil.

As a believer, you have a work to do — a mission and calling. And you need the power of the Holy Spirit overflowing from your life to make you effective.

Jesus said, *"Go ye into all the world, and preach the gospel to every creature."* But He also said, *"And these signs shall follow them that believe; In my name shall they cast out devils; they shall speak with new tongues; they shall take up serpents; and if they drink any deadly thing, it shall not hurt them; they shall lay hands on the sick, and they shall recover"* (Mark 16:15, 17, 18).

Are you a believer? Do you believe that Jesus Christ is the Son of God? Do you believe that what the Bible says is true? Then certain signs are to follow your life. One of them is speaking with "new tongues." Other signs include being able to resist the attacks of Satan and to minister to others.

In other words, you can receive power. That power will help you make...and enable you to help others to make it too! As a believer, you have authority to tell the devil to flee, to cast him out, to lay hands on the sick and see them healed.

Casting down imaginations

But that's not the end of your authority and power through the Holy Spirit. The apostle Paul wrote, *"For though we walk in the flesh, we do not war after the flesh: (For the weapons of our warfare are not carnal, but mighty through God to the pulling down of strong holds;) Casting down imaginations, and every high thing that exalteth itself against the knowledge of God, and bring-*

116

ing into captivity every thought to the obedience of Christ" (2 Corinthians 10:3-5).

The Holy Spirit is your weapon against imaginations, high-sounding reports that oppose God's Word, and thoughts that are not Christ-like. Do you ever have problems with these things?

Does your imagination ever run away from you? Do you think you hear someone trying to break into your house when you're alone at night? Have you ever had a little rash and imagined it was the first symptom of cancer? When you feel a strange twinge of pain, do you imagine you're about to have a heart attack?

Paul says we can cast down those evil imaginations.

One thing that concerns me today is the tremendous influence the news media has on Americans. That bothers me because I know more than ninety percent of reporters and news people are unbelievers — they don't go to church, they doubt the Word of God. Yet, Christians read what they write in the newspaper and listen to what they have to say on radio and television and believe every word.

I meet people who are scared to death about what is going to happen to America. "The TV commentator says the U.S. is doing down the tubes — things really look bad," they say. "Interest rates are too high, prices keep going up, unemployment is breaking the record, you can't buy a house, robbery and murder and violence are increasiing — dear God, we might as well give up!"

But the Word of God says that the Lord's people are going to be taken care of — that they will prosper and be in health.

What do you want to believe — the doom and gloom of the ungodly media or the promises of God? The choice is easy — cast down every high thing that exalteth itself against the knowledge of God.

Then, you need to make your thoughts captive, or subject, to Christ. Refuse to harbor and nurture evil and wicked thinking. You can't keep an impure thought from popping into your mind, but you can surely refuse to dwell on it. If you are troubled with negative thoughts, check up on yourself to see what you are feeding into your mind. What are you reading? What are you watching on TV? As the computer industry says, "garbage in, garbage out."

Fill your mind with good things, uplifting things, encouraging things. Tell yourself, "I am a child of God. He loves me. The Holy Spirit is releasing unlimited power into my life. I can make it!"

One of the most beautiful benefits of the baptism in the Holy Spirit is the increased prayer power it gives you. That alone can be the difference between defeat and success in your life. I love the way the Living Bible says it:

"And in the same way — by our faith — the Holy Spirit helps us with our daily problems and in our praying. For we don't even know what we should pray for, nor how to pray as we should; but the Holy Spirit prays for us with such feeling that it cannot be expressed in words. And the Father who knows all hearts knows, of course, what the Spirit is saying as he pleads for us in harmony with God's own will. And we know that all that happens to us is working for our good if we love God and are fitting into his plans" (Romans 8:26-28).

You need the Holy Spirit's help in your life. I urge you to receive it today. If you have already been baptized in the Holy Spirit, renew your experience and allow Him to work in a greater way in your life.

Begin learning more about the ministry of the Holy Spirit. Did you know that twenty-two out of the thirty-nine books of the Old Testament refer to the Holy

Ghost? It's true. And the New Testament is literally filled with references to Him. There are 261 passages in which the Spirit is directly mentioned. The Gospels contain fifty-six references, the Acts of the Apostles have fifty-seven, the Pauline epistles have 112, and the other books of the New Testament have thirty-six.

So what I'm talking about has plenty of support in God's word. The doctrine of the Holy Spirit is completely scriptural.

The most important thing you can know now is that the Holy Spirit is for you. He is on your side. And no matter what the challenge you have to face, He is with you. You can make it through His unlimited power.

Chapter Ten
How You
Can Make It!

We live in a generation that demands instant gratification. We don't want to wait for anything. We're always in a hurry.

Drivers sit impatiently at traffic lights, and chafe at the speed limit they think slows them down too much. They want to get where they're going as fast as possible.

This is an age of instant everything — from coffee to brown-and-serve rolls to micro-wave TV dinners. If we go out to eat, we're likely to be more interested in the speed of the service than the quality of the food. Our impatience has even spawned an entire new industry that provides an endless variety of so-called fast foods.

So I suppose it's not too surprising that our "instant" mind set has carried over into our Christian life as well. The motto of the modern church seems to be — "In at 11, out by 12!" The congregation slips in and follows the formula — a hymn, a minute of silent prayer, a sermonette, and…"excuse me, I'd like to get out before the rush." It's what I call "zip zap" religion.

There are people around who teach that the proper way to pray for what you need from God is to ask once and never mention it again. You can then act like you've got what you prayed for (and hope it eventually comes), or assume that God didn't want you to have it. If you've really got faith, they say, you'll get your healing *instantly*, the miracle will happen *instantly*, the request will be granted *instantly*.

I suppose that's all right if it works for you. But my track record with instant answers to prayer hasn't been that spectacular. Don't misunderstand me — I'm not saying there is no such thing as an instant healing or and instant miracle. There have been times when God has answered my prayers almost before I could think them! But this certainly hasn't been the norm for me.

And most of the people I've observed trying to live and practice a "zip zap" religion are pretty easy to identify. They call themselves failures! They're the ones who aren't making it!

What, then, is the proper way to pray? What is the secret I have to share on how you can make it?

Try persistence.

Pray with perseverance.

The Bible says, *"Praying always with all prayer and supplication in the Spirit, and watching thereunto with all perseverance and supplication for all saints"* (Ephesians 6:18).

Praying always! Perseverance! Somehow those words don't sound very instant. The truth is, there are no magic rabbit's foot techniques that guarantee the immediate delivery of the blessings of God. It takes patient, determined, persistent faith.

I do not mean to suggest that, as Christians, we must go to extreme lengths to overcome God's reluctance to answer our prayers. He does not withhold any good thing from us. But neither is He a bellboy who comes running at the snap of our fingers.

"I can do all things..."

Someone has suggested — and I tend to agree — that God seldom does for us what we can do ourselves. Og Mandino, in his excellent book, *The Greatest Salesman in the World,* said that rather than praying

121

for material things, he asked for guidance. "Only for guidance will I pray, that I may be shown the way to acquire these things, and my prayer will always be answered."

I do believe that God is interested and concerned about everything that touches our lives. And I am convince that He does bless us with *things,* that He delights in giving us the desire of our hearts. But no less a spiritual authority than the apostle Paul endorsed the concept of individual effort by saying, *"I can do all things through Christ which strengtheneth me"* (Philippians 4:13). Notice that while Christ does the strengthening, we're responsible for the doing!

The Gospel of Luke contains several parables Jesus told to teach important spiritual truths. Two of them deal with the principle of perseverance. Let's look at them, as paraphrased in *The Living Bible:*

One day Jesus told his disciples a story to illustrate their need for constant prayer and to show them that they must keep praying until the answer comes.

"There was a city judge," he said, "a very godless man who had great contempt for everyone.

"A widow of that city came to him frequently to appeal for justice against a man who had harmed her. The judge ignored her for a while, but eventually she got on his nerves.

" 'I fear neither God nor man,' he said to himself, 'but this woman bothers me. I'm going to see that she gets justice, for she is wearing me out with her constant coming!' "

Then the Lord said, "If even an evil judge can be worn down like that, don't you think that God will surely give justice to his people who plead with him day and night? Yes! He will answer them quickly!" (Luke 18:1-8).

The moral to the story is abundantly clear. When we have a need that only God can provide, we are to go and ask for His help. Too often we try to work out our problems on our own — as we should. But if we can't solve the problem, we throw up our hands and quit. We're too easily defeated. We look at the circumstances and just give up. Yet the greatest power on earth is a fraction of a second away. How often do we fail to pray and ask God's help in time of trouble?

If you pray and there seems to be no immediate answer, don't quit. Pray again. Go back to the Lord again and again until you do get an answer.

You may not always get the answer you'd like. Sometimes God says yes. Sometimes He says no. And sometimes He says to wait. But He will always give you an answer...if you persevere. Jesus said that if an evil judge could be worn down by persistent appeals, God would surely answer His people who plead with Him day and night. And seeing their perseverance, He would answer them quickly.

Keep on knocking

The second parable Jesus told is found in Luke 11:
"Suppose you went to a friend's house at midnight, wanting to borrow three loaves of bread. You would shout up to him, 'A friend of mine has just arrived for a visit and I've nothing to give him to eat.' He would call down from the bedroom, 'Please don't ask me to get up. The door is locked for the night and we are all in bed. I just can't help you this time.'

"But I'll tell you this — though he won't do it as a friend, if you keep knocking long enough he will get up and give you everything you want — just because of your persistence. And so it is with prayer — keep on asking and you will keep on getting; keep on looking and you

will keep on finding; knock and the door will be opened" (Luke 11:5-9, *The Living Bible*).

Keep on asking. Keep on looking. Keep on knocking. That's how you can make it. That's the key you can hold on to.

Too often we fail to make it because we knock once very lightly, then get discouraged when no one comes to the door. We allow Satan to whisper in our ear, "Who do you think you are to come to God Almighty with such a puny request? He has more important people than you praying, and you'll have to wait for your answer until He takes care of the big ones." Before long we start to believe the devil's lies — we actually think that God doesn't hear us.

Or we start out to study the Word of God and come across something we don't understand. "That's just too complicated for me," we say, laying the Bible aside. And once again we are defeated because we quit.

A recent poll showed that the average Christian prays less than five minutes a day...and reads the Bible less than five minutes a day. Is it any wonder that the church is full of weak Christians? And how can we hope to have any direction in our lives, a path to walk, a light to lead us if we never go to the power source for direction?

Perseverance is the key. Keep on knocking. Keep on keeping on.

God is calling us as His children to get off of our beds of ease and correct our lackadaisical attitude toward Him. He wants us to be persistent and consistent in reading His Word and to persevere in our prayer life. He wants us to hold on and press through until the answer comes.

Congressman James R. Jones of Oklahoma is an outstanding Christian legislator in the United States

House of Representatives. He serves on the powerful Ways and Means Committee and is chairman of the House Budget Committee. During his campaigns for re-election he often shares his personal philosophy with his constituents: "If we work as though everything depends on us, and pray as though everything depends on God, there is nothing we cannot accomplish."

I like that, don't you? If we do our best, God will do His best for us. And any one believer, with God, is a majority.

Never give up!

In this book I've tried to help you understand that it is God's will for you to succeed...to make it in life. I stressed the importance of your personal salvation as the first thing to get settled. I shared my God-given, Bakker-tested guarantees for success. I tried to help you understand how praising God is the best way out of any valley experience that may come your way. And I shared some practical suggestions on how to make it through sickness, with your finances, with your family, and out of depression. And in the last chapter, we studied together how the Holy Spirit offers unlimited power to help you make it.

This chapter has been devoted to the powerful principle of perseverance. This is really how you can make it. As Dr. Norman Vincent Peale says, "It's always too soon to give up!"

When the great Winston Churchill became Prime Minister of Great Britain, he was invited to give a speech at the school he had attended as a boy. That day the students and teachers assembled and waited expectantly for the great orator to begin.

Members of the press were there to see what great words of wisdom their nation's foremost statesman would offer to the youngsters who would be the leaders of tomorrow.

They would never forget his speech. Churchill walked to the podium and stood silently before his young audience for a long moment, as if weighing what he had to say. Then he began:

"Never give up. NEVER GIVE UP. NEVER, NEVER, NEVER, EVER GIVE UP."

Then he sat down. That was all he needed to say.

And it is the best thing I can say to you now.

Never ever give up!

God will not fail you.

You can make it!